The
IBIZA
Cookbook

EIVISSA

ANNE
SIJMONSBERGEN

PHOTOGRAPHY BY DAVID MUNNS

HarperCollins*Publishers*

FOR IMOGEN EDWARDS-JONES, THE
BEST AND MOST GENEROUS FRIEND A GIRL
COULD EVER HAVE, WITHOUT WHOM
THIS WOULD NOT HAVE HAPPENED.

HarperCollinsPublishers
1 London Bridge Street, London SE1 9GF

www.harpercollins.co.uk

First published by HarperCollinsPublishers 2016

1 3 5 7 9 10 8 6 4 2

Text © Anne Sijmonsbergen 2016
Photography © David Munns 2016
except pages 94, 95 and 132-33 © Andrew Jackson 2016
Design © Smith & Gilmour 2016

Anne Sijmonsbergen asserts the moral right to be identified as the author of this work

A catalogue record of this book is available from the British Library

HB ISBN 978-0-00-816715-8
EB ISBN 978-0-00- 816832-2

Photography direction and initial design concept: Andrew Jackson
Food styling: Lizzie Harris
Prop styling: Victoria Allen

Printed and bound in China

MIX
Paper from
responsible sources
FSC® C007454

FSC
www.fsc.org

FSC™ is a non-profit international organisation established to promote
the responsible management of the world's forests. Products carrying the
FSC label are independently certified to assure consumers that they come
from forests that are managed to meet the social, economic and
ecological needs of present and future generations,
and other controlled sources.

Find out more about HarperCollins and the environment at
www.harpercollins.co.uk/green

CONTENTS

❖❖❖

INTRODUCTION

Ibiza is on the cusp of a food revolution. In recent years the island's traditional farming and fishing culture has been supplemented with a wave of producers making wonderful artisan products and island shops and markets boasting a growing range of fabulous food. Chefs arriving in Ibiza increasingly base their menus around the island's food cycle, showcasing local, seasonal, sustainable ingredients, and local chefs are upping their game, too. Many restaurants grow their own fruits and vegetables and even more buy local organic produce. With such fresh ingredients readily on offer, the island is quickly becoming an international food destination, with its restaurants featuring regularly in the pages of newspapers and lifestyle magazines around the world.

Our tenure at Can Riero, our organic farm on Ibiza, has coincided with this revolution, leading me on a farming, fishing and foraging odyssey to discover the quality and variety of local food on the island. It has introduced me to a host of producers and chefs, native and *extranjeros* (foreigners), who are writing the next chapter of the island's culinary history. *Eivissa* invites you to explore and recreate the flavours of this Mediterranean isle.

⇓ ⇓ ⇓

Ibiza is an island of myth, tradition, contradiction and eccentricity. Its salt flats have attracted a steady stream of visitors, traders and invaders for more than 3000 years. In this time, Phoenician, Punic, Greek, Roman, Moorish and Catalan influences have all contributed to the island's unique character; Ibiza has a distinctive local identity within the autonomous community of the Balearic Islands and Spain as a whole.

Shaped by the competing energies of isolation and integration, Ibicencos developed a tolerant attitude that defines the island to this day – and an intense self-sufficiency. Nobody becomes Ibicenco just by living here, no matter how long they stay. Even mainland Spaniards are outsiders. This is not as paradoxical as it seems: by fiercely guarding their values, Ibicencos absorbed strangers without losing their own identity.

Over the centuries Ibiza fought off pirates and survived slavery, the plague, poverty and Franco. During the Inquisition, and again through the course of World War Two, Ibiza provided refuge for Jews; during the Spanish Civil War it protected Catholic priests and Republicans alike. The stone watch-towers that dot the island date to the days when Ibiza was a target for pirate raids, as do the fortified village churches to which islanders retreated in troubled times.

Through it all, the locals eked out a living from land and sea and built a legacy: the city and villages, churches, farms, miles of stone walls and terraced fields that have created Ibiza's unique indigenous architecture. Moors contributed agricultural innovations, irrigation systems and waterwheels, forming the basis of local farming, and islanders supplemented what they could grow by fishing and herding sheep and goats. *Campo* life is still rustic. Our neighbour is a shepherdess who herds her charges, often with a lamb tucked under one arm. In the autumn her sister-in-law can be seen in a broad hat and long dress, gathering *algarroba* (carob) pods.

When tourists began to arrive on the island's pristine beaches some sixty years ago they brought with them new forms of creativity. Ibiza drew in hippies, artists, rock stars, writers, shamans and healers. Mass tourism coincided with the explosion of electronic music in the 1980s and 90s, and Ibiza's clubs and tolerant culture made it the world's favourite party spot.

However, despite all this interest in their home, the Ibicencos didn't hand over their newly valuable land to foreign developers. Instead, the islanders built restaurants and hotels which they hand down generation by generation, as they do their farms. Tourism brought new opportunities: now the children of fishermen and farmers study law and medicine.

Through it all, Ibicencos' comfortable insularity has allowed them to embrace diversity. Ibiza is home to significant communities of English, German, Dutch, French and Italian expats, and a reasonable-sized dinner party will have conversations going on in half-a-dozen languages; many island children speak three or four.

Like Ibicencos, these expats have a distinctive quality. Regardless of origin, they tend to be creative, curious and adventurous. The island is a magnet for photographers, designers, yogis, musicians, painters, chefs, dancers and alternative therapists. Together they form a flexible, inclusive community defined by self-expression and a desire to live life to the full.

Food plays a critical role in island culture. It is where ancient traditions meet contemporary ideas. It is a communal experience shared by young and old, Ibicenco and *extranjero* alike. Food and cooking are simple, sensual pleasures that embody the best of Ibiza, old and new.

❧ ❧ ❧

Deep in the verdant heart of the Sant Llorenç valley lies Can Riero, a 450-year-old farm (*finca*) situated in the centre of Ibiza's green belt. The farmhouse is perched on a hill surrounded by sweeping terraces planted with olive, citrus, apple, peach, plum and cherry trees. Skirting them are four broad fields that border the old Santa Eulària river. This cool valley has some of the farm's richest soil.

As with most Ibicenco *fincas*, Can Riero's address – '18' – indicates the order in which it was built. It was the 18th house constructed in Sant Joan, the island's most rural municipality. When we arrived here in 2005, just weeks before the birth of our daughter, my husband and I found proof of the house's antiquity in the form of a Dark Ages electrical system consisting of a tiny generator and some optimistic solar panels. When the alarm signalled a power shortage my husband would bolt outside in the wee hours to pull-start the generator. Often in the rain.

In true island style, installing reliable electricity turned into an eight-year odyssey symbolic of the process of transforming Can Riero into an organic farm. My father once said: 'a historic property is not owned but borrowed' – implying the borrower is responsible for leaving it in better shape than it was found. In this spirit we began work at Can Riero, reclaiming fields and trees, repairing dry stone walls, renovating outbuildings and restoring a centuries-old Moorish *noria* (waterwheel) that draws water from one of the three wells on our land.

As newcomers to an ancient farm we had everything to learn: how to identify the trees, what grows best where, when to plant and how to keep an assortment of chickens, ducks, bees, dogs, cats and a kid happy and thriving. It was a wonderful, confusing profusion of commitments.

Developing the farm went hand in glove with exploring local cuisine, history and culture. Every season brought new opportunities to meet local food producers and cooks. Foraging was a revelation: the pleasure and luxury of being able to make something fresh and delicious by just stepping out of the door and picking wild plants was revelatory. The four seasons bring us foraged asparagus, spinach, rocket, garlic, mushrooms and edible flowers.

We now cultivate most of the fruits and vegetables that can be grown on Ibiza: apricots, peaches, cherries, purple plums, grapes, citrus, almonds, walnuts, avocados, peas, beans, garlic, potatoes, onions, chard, spinach, leeks and dozens of varieties of heirloom tomatoes. Much of this organic produce, in particular the tomatoes, supplies some of the top local restaurants and chefs. The rest we eat and preserve, making our own jams, marmalades, pickles, ketchup and chutneys. The abundance is an endless source of culinary inspiration, and Can Riero's kitchen overflows with local ingredients and islanders swapping ideas about how best to transform them into fabulous things to eat.

※ ※ ※

Cooking is one of the rare forms of expression that both evokes and transcends its origin. Many of the recipes in this book are rooted in Ibicenco and Spanish culinary culture and give a glimpse of the island's ancient customs and modern rural life through the timeless ritual of preparing, sharing and enjoying food.

Developed from my journey through Ibiza's food and culture, these recipes are the culmination of years of cooking and swapping ideas and inspiration with many fabulous cooks – family, friends and professionals alike. They reflect my experience of starting from scratch on Can Riero and learning to grow, gather and produce a profusion of wonderful ingredients. Not least, these recipes pay tribute to the artistry and ingenuity of the many island food producers who have shared their wisdom with me.

Historically, Ibicenco cooking was minimalist by necessity. But with the burgeoning local food scene producing fantastic home-produced ingredients, minimal is fabulous. Our ingredients don't need complicated preparation.

Great dishes start with perfect components, and *Eivissa* demonstrates how precise seasoning is critical to enhancing those components. The recipes show how to coax out flavour with thoughtful seasoning, creating dishes with respect for each element, and building delicious bites. Throughout the book my cornerstone flavour quartet – salt, pepper, lemon and vinegar – play a starring role. They make great ingredients shine and redeem those that are less than perfect.

My ethos is simple: flavour is in the detail. Wonderful ingredients and judicious seasoning ensure every element works together for fantastic cooking and eating.

SEASONALITY AND SEASONING

Ibiza has the luxury of a huge variety of local foods which grow year on year. Dedicated local farmers are supplementing staples such as citrus fruits, tomatoes, peppers, squash, cucumber, courgette, aubergine and melons with guava, mango, strawberries and bananas. And producers are adding to the array of fantastic olive oil, cheese, honey, preserves and charcuterie made locally.

This food revolution is not just occuring on Ibiza; farmers' markets, small-farm livestock and artisanal products are increasingly available in towns and cities right across Europe. London itself, like other major British towns and cities, has an abundance of farmers' markets full of British asparagus, apples, berries, potatoes, wild mushrooms, cheeses, cream, sausages, jams and more. Organic vegetable box schemes are another great way for people to benefit from what local farms and producers have to offer. Buying local may take a bit more planning than running to the supermarket, but there are great rewards for making that little bit of effort.

All eat-local people have their own approach to sourcing. At Can Riero it's simple: Ibiza first. We buy as much as we can from the island, then we extend our reach to Catalonia, then Spain, the Mediterranean and Europe. We always buy and eat as much local produce as possible before looking further afield.

Having said that, it is important to keep sight of the joy of food. At Christmas time, when we're months away from cherry season at Can Riero, we indulge in huge, mouthwatering cherries from the southern hemisphere. It's a delicious taste of spring when we need it most. Another guilty pleasure is the Crema Catalana with

Pineapple and Mango (see page 142). Purists may judge, because this isn't a local ingredient, but really it is just too good not to eat every once in a while.

Seasonal eating is often treated as a food trend or novelty, but it is how humans have eaten for millennia. The benefits of eating this way are enormous: food is fresher, more nutritious, cheaper and better for the environment. Buying local supports small farmers, preserves traditional skills and knowledge and maintains green spaces.

Modern food culture is inundated with processed, packaged and shipped food, so it can take a little work to find out what is coming out of the earth when and how best to use it. Start by buying a beautiful seasonal food calendar (or download one) and sticking it on the fridge. Soon the rhythms of growth and harvest will become second nature. Shopping, cooking and dining can be guided by what is fresh, guaranteeing the most delicious produce and most rewarding, sustainable approach to cooking.

Seasonality and seasoning are closely linked. To me, seasoning is the use of salt, pepper and/or an acid such as lemon juice or vinegar to enhance flavour. It is the single most important element of good cooking, and the secret to turning ordinary ingredients into extraordinary dishes.

All vegetables, home grown or farm raised, organic or conventional, need seasoning. The shorter the time and distance between a vegetable leaving the ground and entering the kitchen, the better it will taste and the less seasoning it needs to make its natural goodness shine.

Salt, used correctly, transforms food. To understand how, try this experiment. Peel a cucumber and cut three slices. Leave one unsalted. Salt the other two slices. Eat the unsalted slice immediately – it will be a bit bland. The just-salted slice will have a more intense cucumber flavour. Leave the second salted slice to sit for 20 minutes then try it. Marvellous. By then it will have given up water, condensing the cucumber flavour.

Tomatoes are another vegetable transformed by salt. Slice a tomato into wedges, eat one, put the rest into a bowl and salt them well. Leave them for 10–15 minutes and you will find the taste is transformed. Our local grill restaurant, Balafia, serves the most delicious tomato and onion salad – it's all down to seasoning. Like many *campo* restaurants they grow their own tomatoes, but even ordinary tomatoes become sublime if they are sliced, salted and left to rest for 15 minutes.

At Can Riero we mostly use local Ibiza sea salt, which comes in a range of textures. These are not just cosmetic: each has an ideal cooking use.

🌙 **COARSE SEA SALT**: this is my go-to cooking salt. The texture makes it easy to control the amount in pinches or handfuls. I keep a clip-top canning jar next to the stove to salt water, sauces, soups – anything in which it will dissolve. It is perfect for pickling, dry brining and marinating as it is inexpensive and easy to rinse or knock off.

🌙 **KOSHER SALT**: not quite as coarse as sea salt, it's what I use when I'm away from Ibiza. Readily available, cheap and ideal for a range of uses.

🌙 **FINE SALT**: fabulous on home-made popcorn as it sticks to the kernels better, but not ideal for general cooking. My recipe measurements are based on coarse or kosher salt. Substituting fine salt for coarse salt will make the food too salty.

🌙 **FLAKED SALT**: Maldon or *flor de sal* is gathered by raking the fine upper crust of crystals following evaporation in sea-salt pans. Its intricate flakes stay whole, giving a pleasant crunch. Production is limited compared to ordinary salt, which is reflected in its price tag. As a finishing salt it adds wonderful flavour and makes for gorgeous presentation.

The second element of seasoning is acid: lemon or lime juice, or vinegar. Salt enhances; acid brightens. A teaspoon of sherry vinegar lifts *Samfaina* (see page 195). Lime or lemon juice brightens Watermelon Gazpacho (see page 92) like a taste of summer sun. Acid also cuts the flavour of fat, balancing heavy dishes. Almost every savoury dish benefits from a splash of lemon juice or vinegar.

As with salt, different vinegars elicit different flavours.

🌙 **AGED SHERRY VINEGAR** (*vinagre de Jerez*): this is my top choice for cooking. It's complex, highly acidic and wonderful in a range of dishes and as a salad dressing.

🌙 **RED WINE VINEGAR**: a great basic vinegar for soups, stews and deglazing pans.

🌙 **WHITE WINE VINEGAR**: ideal for pickling, marinating and making hot sauce (see page 284).

🌙 **AGED BALSAMIC VINEGAR**: slightly sweet and less acidic, I use it to intensify the flavour of strawberries, tomatoes, peaches and cherries. It's also a favourite on salads.

A final tip on seasoning
Season lightly and often. *Samfaina* (see page 195) is a great example. It is seasoned three times during preparation, so the vegetables get a flavour boost at each stage of cooking. The end result: a more flavourful, better-balanced dish.

SHAPING THE WHITE ISLAND: SALT'S ROLE IN IBIZA'S HISTORY

Salt is perhaps the most important mineral in human history. It is certainly the one that is most essential to Ibiza culture, commerce and cuisine.

The Phoenicians colonised Ibiza some 2800 years ago, they were the first to harvest white gold from the island's salt flats (Ses Salines). They were succeeded by Carthaginians, then the Romans, who harvested Ibicenco salt for 350 years until the fall of their empire. Subsequently, the island's precious natural resource passed through the hands of the Vandals and Byzantines to the Moors.

Ibiza owes much of its distinctive architecture, agriculture and culture to more than three centuries of Moorish rule. It was they who maintained and operated the saltworks that had been in existence for over a millennium. When the Catalans conquered Ibiza in 1235 they designated the salt pans as public property and profits from the salt trade were used to fund local government and defence.

Salt was harvested and transported by hand for hundreds of years. In the heat of late summer and September, workers raked up crystallised salt, piled it into tightly woven baskets and carried it by hand to boats waiting at the shore. Refinements over time included loading docks to accommodate bigger vessels and then, in the late 1800s, industrial machinery, including steam-powered mills to regulate the flow of water through the salt pans.

Thanks to mechanisation, working in the salt pans is no longer a common way to make a living in Ibiza, but salt still contributes more than jobs to the island's economy and culture. Salt is an instantly recognisable local product and, in the hands of cooks, transforms local ingredients into fabulous dishes. From the traditional Ibicenco housewarming gift of bread, salt and wine, to the delicious crunch of salt crystals on *Pan con Tomate* (see page 285), Ibiza's salt is what gives the white island its flavour.

SPRING

Spring on Ibiza is a luxuriously long affair that begins with the emergence of the silvery-pink almond blossoms in mid-February – the first hint of the gorgeous explosion of wild flowers that dominates the island's landscape – and continues until the beginning of June. Gradually the vibrant green of winter comes alive like a scene in an Impressionist painting, changing colour as new flowers come into season, filling the *campo* with yellow Spanish broom, orange poppies and magenta and purple wild gladioli.

Our food is equally fresh and vibrant. Ibiza is a veritable cornucopia of vegetables, fruit, edible flowers and herbs, both cultivated and foraged. All are perfectly evoked by the peppery edible nasturtiums that line Can Riero's stone walls, decorating them with daubs of vivid orange and yellow. Hearty and prolific, once planted these flowers come back stronger and more vigorous every year.

Can Riero's fields are in full production in spring, yielding fresh garlic, onions and leeks, peas, artichokes, green beans, broad beans, lettuces, chard and, our favourite, asparagus. We still have oranges, lemons and grapefruit at their sun-kissed sweetest but our flavour palette shifts from winter's warm spices with citrus to fresh herbs such as coriander, chives and mint which we use as accents or in combination with citrus and salad leaves. Spring foraging is the most plenteous of the year, with wild asparagus, edible flowers, rocket and garlic ready for the picking. This abundance fills our kitchen with inimitable shapes, colours and culinary inspiration.

Toasted bread is the perfect base to show off the tender, young spring vegetables. Complement them with fresh herbs and strong cheeses but keep it simple: two, or at most three, vegetables per tostada is enough. You don't want too many flavours. Try one combination, or make all three for a nice assortment. These tostadas make great bites for guests as they arrive, to serve as starters or as accompaniments to soup for a light lunch. Prepare extra vegetables to use in salads, as side dishes, or on pasta for a second meal.

WILD ROCKET, MOZZARELLA AND SPRING HERB VINAIGRETTE TOSTADAS

Serves 6

Tostadas
3 tbsp extra virgin olive oil
2 pinches salt
12 slices white country bread

Topping
⅓ head wild garlic or
    2–3 regular garlic cloves
80ml (3¼fl oz) extra virgin
    olive oil
Small handful basil
Small handful coriander
Small handful flat-leaf parsley
½ tsp sherry vinegar
70g (3oz) mozzarella, shredded
    into large strips
50g (2oz) wild rocket
Salt and black pepper

To make the tostadas, combine the olive oil and salt in a bowl and brush it over both sides of the bread. Toast the bread on a hot griddle pan, barbecue grill or under the oven grill, until golden. For beautiful, clean char marks, place the bread carefully on the griddle or barbecue grill and do not move it for 2–3 minutes, until golden and toasted. Turn the bread over and place it back on the grill, lining up the grill marks in the same direction as the previous side. Remove, stack up and set aside until the vegetables are ready for assembly.

To make the topping, chop the wild garlic and add it to the olive oil. If you are using regular garlic, slice it finely and macerate it in the oil for 30 minutes, then remove the garlic and discard. Put the garlicky olive oil in a high-sided measuring jug, add the herbs, season with salt and pepper and add a drizzle of vinegar. Blend with a hand-held blender until you have a coarse-textured mixture. Arrange the mozzarella strips on the toast. Add the rocket and drizzle liberally with the herb vinaigrette.

Pea, Courgette and Broad Bean Tostadas with Mahón Curado

❧ ❧ ❧ ❧ ❧ ❧ ❧ ❧ ❧ ❧ ❧

400g (14oz) fresh peas, shelled
600g (1¼lb) fresh baby broad beans, shelled
2 tbsp extra virgin olive oil, plus extra to finish
200g (7oz) courgettes, trimmed and sliced into small batons
50g (2oz) Mahón curado or Pecorino cheese, shaved
Salt and black pepper

❧ ❧ ❧ ❧ ❧ ❧ ❧ ❧ ❧ ❧ ❧

Make the tostadas as before.

Fill a small bowl with ice and water.

Bring 120ml (4½fl oz) water to the boil in a small frying pan with a pinch of salt and add the shelled peas and broad beans. Return to the boil and cook for 3–4 minutes until *al dente,* or until the water evaporates. Tip the vegetables immediately into the iced water to stop them cooking and to set the vibrant green colour. Drain, then set the peas and beans aside in a small bowl. Peel the thin skin from the broad beans and discard.

Rinse out the frying pan, place it over a medium-high heat until hot, add the oil, and heat again for 1 minute. Add the courgette batons to the hot pan and fry for 3–4 minutes until golden, shaking the pan over the burner. Add the peas and double-podded broad beans with a splash of oil and toss to coat. Season lightly with salt and pepper.

Scoop the vegetables onto the tostadas and top with shaved Mahón or Pecorino cheese to serve.

Courgette and Asparagus Tostadas with Ricotta and Mint

❧ ❧ ❧ ❧ ❧ ❧ ❧ ❧ ❧ ❧ ❧

150g (5oz) courgettes, trimmed and cut lengthways into thin ribbons
150g (5oz) thin asparagus spears (or thicker asparagus trimmed and quartered lengthways)
1 tbsp extra virgin olive oil, plus extra for brushing
2 tsp lemon juice
65g (2¾oz) ricotta cheese
Grated zest of ⅓ lemon
Small handful mint leaves, torn
Salt and black pepper

❧ ❧ ❧ ❧ ❧ ❧ ❧ ❧ ❧ ❧ ❧

Make the tostadas as before.

Brush the courgette ribbons and wild asparagus spears with lightly salted olive oil.

Heat a griddle pan over a high heat and grill the asparagus for 3–4 minutes until *al dente.* Turn them halfway through the cooking time, keeping the grill marks neat. Alternatively, brush the spears with olive oil and cook them for 3–4 minutes on a baking tray under a hot grill, turning them once halfway through the cooking time.

Transfer the grilled asparagus to a bowl and toss with the olive oil, 1 teaspoon of the lemon juice and a pinch of salt and pepper, then grill the courgette ribbons for 1–2 minutes on each side and add them to the bowl with the asparagus.

Mix the ricotta with the lemon zest and add the remaining lemon juice and salt and pepper to taste.

Scoop the ricotta onto the tostadas and top with the vegetables. Sprinkle with torn mint leaves and freshly ground pepper.

A long-time Can Riero favourite, we used to make this soup by the barrelful in the spring, to include in our Can Riero organic vegetable boxes. It was the perfect way to use the abundance of cucumbers at peak season, and a lovely extra to offer our clients while they waited for the summer's tomato crop to ripen.

CHILLED CUCUMBER SOUP

Serves 6–8

600g (1¼lb) plain, full-fat
    bio yoghurt
240g (8½oz) crème fraîche
6 pickling cucumbers, peeled,
    or 3 large cucumbers, peeled,
    deseeded and chopped
½ sweet white onion, chopped
1 fresh green jalapeño chilli,
    deseeded and chopped
3 tsp salt
1½ tsp ground black pepper
2 tbsp lemon juice
Small handful chopped chives,
    to serve

Place the yoghurt, crème fraîche, cucumbers, onion, chilli, salt and pepper in a large jug or bowl and purée with a hand-held blender until smooth. Chill for at least 2 hours.

Stir in the lemon juice just before serving and top with cracked black pepper and chopped chives.

We grow ten varieties of citrus fruits at Can Riero, four of which are oranges. The oranges are sweetest in the late winter and early spring, when imported tomatoes are at their worst, which led to me using oranges in salads. Like a good tomato, they are juicy, fresh, slightly acidic and pair well with vinaigrette.

CITRUS SALADS

Serves 4

Blood Orange and Peix Sec Salad

❦❦❦❦❦❦❦❦❦❦❦

¼ red onion, sliced paper thin
3 tbsp extra virgin olive oil
1 tsp sherry vinegar
150g (5oz) mixed lettuce leaves, torn
2 blood oranges, peeled and sliced into rounds
1 large ripe avocado, peeled, stoned and
    sliced into 8 wedges
90g (3½oz) peix sec (dried fish in Catalan),
    drained, or Italian bottarga
Small handful microgreens
30g (1¼oz) toasted walnuts, roughly chopped
4 tbsp blood orange juice
Salt and black pepper

❦❦❦❦❦❦❦❦❦❦❦

Place the onion slices in a bowl of ice-cold water and leave to soak for 20 minutes, then drain and pat dry.

To make the dressing, put the oil, vinegar and a pinch of salt in a jar. Seal with a lid and shake well to combine. Toss the lettuce leaves with 1 tablespoon of the dressing and place a handful of dressed lettuce on each plate.

Divide the orange segments, avocado and onion among the plates and top with the Peix Sec. Garnish with the microgreens and walnuts then drizzle with the remaining dressing and orange juice. Season and serve immediately.

Blood Orange, Carrot, Mint and Spring Onion Salad

❦❦❦❦❦❦❦❦❦❦❦

½ small red onion, sliced paper thin
6 carrots, peeled and coarsely grated
2 blood oranges, peeled and segmented
Small handful spearmint or peppermint leaves,
    cut into ribbons
1 tbsp blood orange juice
Handful yellow cucumber blossoms,
    or other edible flowers
Handful microgreens

Dressing
3 tbsp extra virgin olive oil
1 tsp sherry vinegar
Pinch ground or freshly grated nutmeg
Salt and black pepper

❦❦❦❦❦❦❦❦❦❦❦

Prepare the onion slices as before.

Put all of the dressing ingredients in a jar, seal with a lid and shake to combine.

Combine the grated carrots, orange segments and onion slices in a salad bowl. Toss with 1½ tablespoons of the dressing, season and toss again. Add the mint leaves and orange juice and toss once more. Adjust the seasoning if necessary, adding more dressing if desired.

Serve on a platter scattered with edible flowers and microgreens.

FISH TREE

Formentera's fishermen have been sun-drying their excess catch in the same way for centuries. In Port de Sa Savina there is a *sabina* (juniper) cut, stripped, dried and set up as a communal drying rack. The ancient structure weathers the intense sun and winter rains beautifully – nobody knows how long the current one has been in place, but it has been many, many years.

Fisherman David Sánchez and his family carry on this tradition with peix sec ('dried fish' in Catalan) preserved in olive oil. The fish is cleaned, cut into strips, soaked in brine and hung out to dry. When fully cured, it is hand-shredded into smaller pieces and packed in oil. Government sanitation standards now require that David use a drying room, but the local fishermen still use the remaining *sabinas* in Formentera's ports.

ARTICHOKES

Artichokes are one of Ibiza's great spring pleasures. Simply served with Maltaise (page 281) or vinaigrette for dipping, poached in olive oil with wild herbs, or stuffed and roasted, artichokes are a statement vegetable. Trimming and preparing them can take a bit of time, but the results are extraordinary.

There are two basic ways to prepare artichokes, depending on how they are to be eaten.

Preparing artichokes for stuffing
For stuffed artichokes (see recipe pages 39–40), or to simply boil, bake or steam them, preparation is straightforward. Wash them well under cold running water using a soft vegetable brush. Prepare a large bowl of cold water and squeeze in the juice of a lemon, adding the lemon halves. Top and tail the artichoke with a large, sharp knife, cutting off about 2cm (¾in) from the top and 1-2cm (½–¾in) from the stem if boiling or steaming. It is a good idea to slice the stem off at the base so it will sit upright in the pan and trim the thorny ends of the leaves with kitchen shears for neater presentation. Work into the flower with your fingers, gently opening the leaves to create space for the stuffing. Drop the prepared artichokes into lemon water until they are needed, to preserve their colour.

Trimming artichokes
Recipes such as Crispy Fried Artichoke Hearts (see page 36) call for a bit more preparation. Prepare a bowl of cold lemon water, as before, then cut the stem, leaving about 3cm (1¼in) of stalk. Cut off the top of the flower about a third of the way down, leaving about 3cm (1¼in) of artichoke above the base of the stem. Break off the tough outer leaves then use a sharp paring knife to cut away the remaining outer leaves and any fibrous bits. The artichoke should now be the shape of a golf tee. In the centre of the cup is the fuzzy 'choke'. Scoop this out with a spoon, taking care to remove it completely – this inedible fuzz will ruin a dish. Once prepared, drop the artichoke into the lemon water.

❦ ❦ ❦

Tip: Small Ibicenco artichokes don't need to have their choke removed.

This recipe uses the huge yield of artichokes we get on the island. Make a big batch of these hearts: they store well in a jar in the fridge, covered with oil. Use in salads, or serve as antipasto or with cheese. However you decide to eat them, they're heaven.

CRISPY FRIED ARTICHOKE HEARTS

Makes 48 pieces

❧ ❧ ❧ ❧ ❧ ❧ ❧ ❧ ❧ ❧ ❧

Juice of 2 lemons (reserve
    the halves)
12 artichokes, trimmed and
    prepared (see page 34)
Extra virgin olive oil
Handful rosemary sprigs
Handful thyme sprigs
Handful sage leaves
1 head garlic, cloves peeled
    and crushed
2 whole dried chillies, halved
    lengthways and deseeded
Small handful black peppercorns
Pared strips of peel from 1 lemon

Fill a bowl with water and add the lemon juice and two of the lemon halves to stop the artichokes turning brown.

Take the prepared artichokes and, using a paring knife, peel the stem until you reach the inner circle (where the woody bit ends). Peel the base, leaving the heart intact. Cut each trimmed artichoke heart into quarters and immediately put them in the lemon water. Drain, dry with a tea towel and place in a large saucepan, cut-side down. Add olive oil to cover, then add the rosemary, thyme, sage, garlic, chillies, peppercorns and lemon peel to the pan. Bring the artichokes to a gentle simmer over a medium heat, reduce the heat to low, cover and simmer gently for 20–25 minutes.

When the artichokes are *al dente* increase the heat to high. Fry for 5–6 minutes, turning the hearts with tongs so they crisp up evenly. The artichokes should be dark golden and evenly crisped. Remove the pan from the heat and leave the artichoke hearts in the pan to cool. Serve immediately at just above room temperature, or store in sterilised jars, adding olive oil to completely cover.

Lamb and artichoke make a winning combination; the sweetness of the onion softens the metallic note of the artichoke, bringing it all together.

SPICED LAMB-STUFFED ARTICHOKE

Serves 4

❦ ❦ ❦ ❦ ❦ ❦ ❦ ❦ ❦ ❦ ❦

2 tbsp extra virgin olive oil, plus extra for drizzling and frying
1 onion, halved lengthways and thinly sliced
2 garlic cloves, crushed
75g (3oz) breadcrumbs
350g (12oz) minced lamb
¼ tsp cumin seeds
¼ tsp coriander seeds
1 fresh cayenne chilli, deseeded and finely chopped
4 tbsp red wine
Handful baby spinach leaves, roughly chopped
1 tsp grated lemon zest
1 tsp lemon juice
Small handful mint, leaves roughly chopped
Small handful flat-leaf parsley, leaves roughly chopped
120ml (4½fl oz) white wine
8 small or 4 globe artichokes, trimmed and prepared for stuffing (see page 34)
Salt and black pepper

❦ ❦ ❦

Tip: The above cooking time is for medium-sized artichokes. If using small, test at 45 minutes; if using the larger globe artichokes, test at 75 minutes.

Heat the olive oil in a heavy-based saucepan over a medium-high heat. Add the onion and garlic, reduce the heat to medium-low and fry, uncovered, for 8–10 minutes until the onion is soft and golden.

Meanwhile, toast the breadcrumbs in a frying pan with 1 tablespoon of oil for 2–3 minutes, until golden. Remove from the heat and set aside.

Add the lamb, cumin and coriander seeds and chilli to the fried onion. Increase the heat to medium and fry for 5–6 minutes, until the lamb is nearly cooked through, then push the lamb to one side and deglaze the pan with the red wine, scraping up the flavourful bits stuck to the bottom. When the wine has nearly evaporated add the spinach and cook until the liquid from the spinach evaporates. Add the toasted breadcrumbs, stir through and fry for 1 minute to incorporate. Remove from the heat and allow to cool slightly, then stir in the lemon zest and juice, mint and parsley. Season to taste and mix well.

Preheat the oven to 160°C (320°F), gas mark 3. Pour the white wine into a high-sided baking tray and heat it in the oven.

Remove the artichokes from the lemon water. Stuff the artichokes with the lamb mixture, starting at the middle then stuffing the outer layers between the leaves. Put the stuffed artichokes in the heated baking tray with the wine. Drizzle them with olive oil and cover the tray with foil. Bake in the oven for 55–60 minutes, checking on them occasionally and adding more wine if needed. Pierce the centre of an artichoke with a skewer to test if it's tender. When the heart is just yielding, remove the foil and bake for a further 15–20 minutes, until the liquid has evaporated, then test it again – the heart should be completely yielding and the outer leaves crispy. Remove from the oven and serve.

Fennel-Stuffed Artichoke

Fennel and artichoke are a classic marriage and one of my favourite food pairings – just delicious.

❦ ❦ ❦ ❦ ❦ ❦ ❦ ❦ ❦ ❦ ❦

3–4 tbsp extra virgin olive oil
1 onion, chopped
1 garlic clove, crushed
1 fennel bulb, trimmed and finely chopped
¼ tsp fennel seeds, toasted and ground
    in mortar and pestle
60ml (2½fl oz) white wine
60g (2½oz) breadcrumbs
60g (2½oz) Manchego semi-curado
    or mature Cheddar cheese, grated
8 small or 4 globe artichokes, trimmed
    and prepared for stuffing (see page 34)
120ml (4½fl oz) white wine
Salt and black pepper

❦ ❦ ❦ ❦ ❦ ❦ ❦ ❦ ❦ ❦ ❦

Heat 2 tablespoons of the olive oil in a heavy-based saucepan, add the onion and garlic and fry for 8–10 minutes until soft and golden. Add the chopped fennel, ground fennel seeds and white wine, stir to combine, then season with salt and pepper. Cover and cook for 6–7 minutes until the liquid has been absorbed. Add another tablespoon of olive oil and fry for a further 3–4 minutes until the fennel is completely soft.

Meanwhile, toast the breadcrumbs in a frying pan with 2 teaspoons of olive oil for 2–3 minutes, until golden. Remove from the heat and add them to the vegetable mixture, then cook for a further 3–4 minutes, until the breadcrumbs are well combined with the vegetables. Remove the saucepan from the heat and add the cheese. Season to taste and mix well. Stuff the prepared artichokes and bake as on page 39.

Swiss Chard-Stuffed Artichoke

Pungent, wild Swiss chard works beautifully with artichokes, while the crème fraîche smoothes out the flavour.

❦ ❦ ❦ ❦ ❦ ❦ ❦ ❦ ❦ ❦ ❦

3 tbsp extra virgin olive oil
2 shallots, finely chopped
2 garlic cloves, crushed
Small handful thyme, leaves finely chopped
60ml (2½fl oz) white wine
200g (7oz) Swiss chard, finely chopped
2 tbsp crème fraîche
60g (2½oz) breadcrumbs
2 Roasted Tomatoes (see page 275), chopped
3–4 anchovies in oil, drained and finely chopped
8 small or 4 globe artichokes, trimmed and
    prepared for stuffing (see page 34)
60g (2½oz) Mahón curado or Pecorino cheese, grated
120ml (4½fl oz) white wine
Salt and black pepper

❦ ❦ ❦ ❦ ❦ ❦ ❦ ❦ ❦ ❦ ❦

Heat 2 tablespoons of the olive oil in a heavy-based saucepan, add the shallots and garlic and fry for 8–10 minutes, until soft and golden. Add the thyme and white wine and stir to combine, then season with salt and pepper. Add the Swiss chard and crème fraîche and cook for 6–7 minutes until the leaves are soft and slightly reduced.

Meanwhile, toast the breadcrumbs in a frying pan in the remaining olive oil for 2–3 minutes, until golden. Remove from the heat and set aside.

Add the roasted tomatoes, breadcrumbs and anchovies to the vegetables and mix well. Remove from the heat and season to taste. Stuff the prepared artichokes and bake as on page 39. When you remove the foil, sprinkle the artichokes with the grated cheese then bake for the final 15–20 minutes.

This version of the fabulous Spanish classic is adapted from the tortilla made by Ibiza's tortilla masters at Restaurant Can Cosmi, a family-run restaurant at the edge of the gorgeous, almond tree-filled valley of Santa Agnès. Can Cosmi, which started out in the 1950s as a shop and bar, has been turning out the very best tortillas for decades. Tortilla is way too delicious to just stick to the classic. Once you've mastered the technique, the possibilities are endless.

CLASSIC TORTILLA

Serves 6

❦ ❦ ❦ ❦ ❦ ❦ ❦ ❦ ❦ ❦ ❦ ❦

240ml (9fl oz) extra virgin olive oil, plus 2 tbsp (if needed)
1kg (2lb 2oz) potatoes, peeled and cut into 1 x 2cm (½ x ¾in) lengths
3 large onions (about 900g/2lb) halved and sliced into 0.5cm (¼in) thick half moons
¼ red pepper, deseeded and cut into 2cm (¾in) cubes
¼ green pepper, deseeded and cut into 2cm (¾in) cubes
12 eggs, beaten together
Salt and black pepper

❦ ❦ ❦

Tip: Be careful not to burn the bottom of the tortilla before cooking it through. If you think the tortilla might burn, lower the heat and pull the pan on and off the heat as necessary.

Heat the oil in a large, heavy-based, non-stick frying pan over a medium heat to 180°C (350°F). Carefully add half the potatoes and fry them for 8–10 minutes, until golden. Remove with a slotted spoon and transfer to a plate lined with kitchen paper. Reheat the oil and repeat with the remaining potatoes. Drain well, allow to cool slightly then cut into chunks and set aside.

Pour off two-thirds of the oil, heat the remaining oil and fry the onions and peppers for 8–10 minutes until soft. Stir in the potatoes and cook for 5–6 minutes over a medium heat.

With the pan over the heat, spread the vegetables into an even layer. Sprinkle with salt and pepper then pour over the eggs. Using a rubber- or silicone-tipped spatula, gently loosen the egg around the rim. If it is cooking too quickly, reduce the heat to medium-low. Cook for 1–2 minutes, until the edge of the tortilla begins to set, then pull it away from the rim and tilt the pan so liquid egg fills the space. Repeat, working all the way around the pan to keep the tortilla even, until all the egg is set (about 7–8 minutes). The top of the tortilla will be wet but should be cooked at least halfway through. Cover the pan with a plate slightly larger than the pan. Using oven gloves, hold the pan and invert the tortilla onto the plate in one quick motion.

Add the 2 tablespoons of olive oil to the pan if it is dry and place over a medium heat. Carefully slide the tortilla back into the pan, wet side down, and reduce the heat to medium-low. Move the spatula around the rim, tucking under any rough tortilla edge so it is neat and rounded. Cook for 6–8 minutes, until the tortilla is slightly springy to the touch.

Remove from the heat and invert the tortilla onto a clean plate. Rest for 10 minutes (it will continue to cook).

Roasted Tomato, Goat's Cheese and Chive Tortilla

This roasted tomato version is a Can Riero favourite. The tomatoes add flavourful moisture and the cheese gives the tortilla a lovely creamy tang.

❦ ❦ ❦ ❦ ❦ ❦ ❦ ❦ ❦ ❦ ❦ ❦

4 tbsp extra virgin olive oil
3 large onions (about 900g/2lb), halved and sliced into 0.5cm (¼in) thick half moons
800g (1¾lb) Roasted Tomatoes (see page 275), drained and cut into thin strips lengthways
Large handful chives, snipped
12 eggs, beaten together
250g (9oz) soft goat's cheese, crumbled
Salt and black pepper

❦ ❦ ❦ ❦ ❦ ❦ ❦ ❦ ❦ ❦ ❦

Heat the oil in a large, non-stick frying pan then add the onions and cook for 25–30 minutes over a low heat until they are soft, golden and sweet. Do not let them stick to the bottom of the pan or the tortilla will also stick.

Spread the onions out over the bottom of the pan, add the roasted tomatoes and sprinkle with the chives, creating an even layer of vegetables in the bottom of the pan. Sprinkle liberally with salt and pepper. Pour in the eggs, distributing them evenly over the vegetables, then scatter over the goat's cheese and gently submerge it in the eggs so the tortilla does not stick when flipped. Continue cooking, following the method on page 43.

Serrano Ham, Pea and Mint Tortilla

This Serrano and pea tortilla variation is another Ibiza speciality. Replace the potatoes with an equal amount of peas, making for intense pea flavour. The mint is my addition; it lifts the flavour, I just love the combination of peas, mint and ham.

❦ ❦ ❦ ❦ ❦ ❦ ❦ ❦ ❦ ❦ ❦ ❦

1.5kg (3lb 4oz) whole fresh peas, shelled (about 1kg/2lb 2oz)
4 tbsp extra virgin olive oil
3 large onions (about 900g/2lb), halved and sliced into 0.5cm (¼in) thick half moons
150g (5oz) Serrano Reserva ham, cut into thin strips
Small handful mint leaves, cut into ribbons
12 eggs, beaten together
Salt and black pepper

❦ ❦ ❦ ❦ ❦ ❦ ❦ ❦ ❦ ❦ ❦

Bring a saucepan of water to the boil, add the peas and cook for 2–3 minutes until tender, then drain and plunge the peas into a bowl of iced water to stop them cooking and set the colour.

Fry the onions in the olive oil following the classic method (left), then add the Serrano ham and fry for 3–4 minutes until slightly crisp. Add the peas and toss to combine and coat them in the oil.

Spread the peas, ham and onions out in an even layer on the bottom of the pan, sprinkle with the mint, plenty of pepper and a little salt. Pour the eggs over and continue cooking, following the method on page 43.

ASPARAGUS

On Ibiza wild asparagus is the first sign of the arrival of spring. The spears line ancient stone walls from March until the end of April. And what a treat it is! Thinner and less sweet than its cultivated cousin, wild asparagus has a concentrated flavour that comes from a life lived wholly by the rules of nature. On Sundays in particular, the *campo* is thick with foragers searching along the sides of roads and small dirt tracks, across fields and along stone walls. Strangely, it is not uncommon to find the bottoms of snapped-off spears just a few metres from the Can Riero farmhouse. Who are these people and how do they go undetected?

Never mind, there is plenty for everyone and we have learned to pick on Saturdays. Several years ago, encouraged by the abundance of the wild stuff, we planted several rows and now enjoy both native and cultivated asparagus throughout spring.

Wild or not, freshly picked asparagus is heaven. You can use tender young spears raw in the following recipes for a more intense flavour.

How to cook perfect asparagus
Bring 60ml (2½fl oz) of water to a rapid boil in a large frying pan. Add the asparagus and ½ teaspoon salt. Cook the wild asparagus spears for 2–3 minutes until *al dente*, tossing them gently with rubber- or silicone-tipped tongs. Regular asparagus needs to cook for 5–6 minutes until *al dente*. Pour away any remaining water – the pan will be streaked with the evaporated salt. Pour in 2 tablespoons of extra virgin olive oil, toss to coat the pan in the oil, then fry the asparagus over a high heat for 1–2 minutes, until the spears are evenly coated with salt and oil.

❧ ❧ ❧

Tip: Snap off the bottoms of shop-bought spears and place them in a container with a little water and a large pinch of sugar. Absorbing the water restores moisture and some of the just-picked freshness.

The combination of asparagus, Serrano ham and egg is divine
and you can serve it any time: it's great for breakfast, brunch,
lunch or a light supper. Poached egg is an elegant variation – as is
white truffle oil – it isn't Spanish, but sometimes the ethos of
eating local produce has to give way to a perfect culinary pairing.

ASPARAGUS WITH SERRANO HAM AND EGG

Serves 4

✤ ✤ ✤ ✤ ✤ ✤ ✤ ✤ ✤ ✤ ✤

2 tsp extra virgin olive oil,
    plus extra for drizzling
75g (3oz) Serrano ham slices,
    halved lengthways
6 eggs
750g (1lb 10oz) asparagus
    (about 20 spears), cooked
    as on page 46
White truffle oil (optional)
Black pepper

Heat the olive oil in a frying pan over a medium heat, add the
Serrano ham and fry for 1–2 minutes until crispy. Remove from
the heat.

To medium-boil the eggs, place them in a large saucepan of
cold water and bring to the boil. Remove from the heat and leave
for 1½–2 minutes, then transfer the eggs to a bowl of cold water
to stop the cooking process. Peel, rinse off any remaining shell,
and quarter the eggs. The yolks should be set and a bit opaque,
but not runny.

To serve, arrange about 5 cooked asparagus spears, 6 egg
quarters and a few strips of crispy ham on each plate. Dress
with olive or white truffle oil and pepper.

✤ ✤ ✤

Tip: Taste before adding extra salt, as frying the Serrano
ham brings out its saltiness.

Asparagus, Beans and Rocket with Lemon Ricotta

What a beautiful spring dish this is. The combination of two beans makes for great flavour and texture. Adding plenty of salt to the cooking water and plunging the beans in iced water helps retain their vivid colour.

❀ ❀ ❀ ❀ ❀ ❀ ❀ ❀ ❀ ❀ ❀

400g (14oz) thin, young green beans, topped and tailed
1kg (2lb 2oz) fresh baby broad beans, shelled
2 tbsp olive oil, plus extra for drizzling
1 tsp lemon juice
300g (11oz) fresh ricotta
Finely grated zest of 1 lemon
100g (3½oz) rocket
750g (1lb 10oz) asparagus (about 20 spears), cooked as on page 46
20g (¾oz) Mahón curado or Parmesan cheese, grated
Salt and black pepper

❀ ❀ ❀ ❀ ❀ ❀ ❀ ❀ ❀ ❀ ❀

Boil a medium saucepan of water, add ½ teaspoon of salt and the green beans. Blanch for 1-2 minutes, remove with tongs, and plunge into a bowl of cold water. Return the water in the pan to the boil and add the broad beans. Cook for 3-4 minutes until *al dente*, drain and leave to dry on a tea towel until they are cool enough to peel away the thin membrane. Toss the broad and green beans together with 1 tablespoon of the oil and lemon juice and season with salt and pepper.

Mix the ricotta in a bowl with most of the lemon zest and season.

Toss the rocket with the remaining olive oil and a pinch of salt. Divide among 4 plates. Top each with the asparagus, beans, plus a dollop of lemon ricotta. Dress with more oil, season with pepper, sprinkle over the cheese and the remaining lemon zest.

Asparagus and Crab Salad

Asparagus and crab is yet another terrific combination. Keeping it very simple allows the flavours to shine.

❀ ❀ ❀ ❀ ❀ ❀ ❀ ❀ ❀ ❀ ❀

1 tbsp extra virgin olive oil, plus extra for drizzling
750g (1lb 10oz) asparagus (about 20 spears), cooked as on page 46
150g (5oz) cooked fresh white crab meat, or good-quality tinned crab meat, drained
Handful chives, snipped, including flowers
1 lemon, cut into 4 wedges
Salt and black pepper

❀ ❀ ❀ ❀ ❀ ❀ ❀ ❀ ❀ ❀ ❀

Arrange a quarter of the cooked asparagus spears on each plate, together with the crab meat. Dress with olive oil, season with salt and pepper and sprinkle with chives. Serve with lemon wedges.

Cheese platters are wonderful for entertaining. We make frequent use of them at Can Riero for people popping in for a quick glass of wine, a light supper with an interesting salad or as a precursor to (or final course for) a large farm dinner.

SPRING CHEESE PLATTER WITH PICKLED GREEN TOMATOES

Serves 4

❧ ❧ ❧ ❧ ❧ ❧ ❧ ❧ ❧ ❧ ❧ ❧

150g (5oz) soft goat's cheese
200g (7oz) Mahón semi-curado
100g (3½oz) almonds, toasted
  and salted
150g (5oz) Serrano Reserva ham
200g (7oz) Manchego curado
Pickled Green Tomatoes
  (see below)
150g (5oz) breadsticks
10 slices rustic white bread
300g (10oz) fresh cherries

❧ ❧ ❧ ❧ ❧ ❧ ❧ ❧ ❧ ❧ ❧

Pickled Green Tomatoes
You will need: 2 x 1 litre
  (1¾ pints) sterilised preserving
  jars with lids (see page 295)

2kg (4lb 4oz) fully grown,
  green unripe tomatoes
250g (9oz) coarse sea salt
1 litre (1¾ pints) white vinegar
1.5kg (3lb 4oz) caster sugar
4 tbsp whole allspice berries
2 tbsp whole cloves
4 whole star anise
3 tbsp whole black peppercorns
2 cinnamon sticks, broken in half

Flavour, texture, colour and variety are the elements to keep in mind when composing a great plate of food. Start by choosing a seasonal fruit as the central flavour and work everything else around it – fruit is great because not only does it visually mark the season, but it is also sweet and adds fabulous colour to the platter. Nuts add texture – choose ones that complement the flavour of the fruit: almonds with cherries, for example. Choose an odd number of cheeses: either three or five depending on the size of the party. The cheeses should work well with the other elements. Here, the goat's cheese and the Mahón work well with the cherries and the almonds. Aim to have a goat's or sheep's milk variety (or two) as well as a cow's milk cheese. Cured meat adds rich flavour: choose one that works well with the rest of the elements.

Finish the platter with a homemade pickle or chutney to provide some acidity and cut the richness of the cheese. The Pickled Green Tomatoes make a perfect pairing with both the Serrano ham and the Manchego.

PICKLED GREEN TOMATOES
Cut the tomatoes into 1cm (½in) thick slices and layer them with the sea salt in a large stainless-steel bowl. Set aside at room temperature for 4 hours.

Rinse the tomatoes 2–3 times to remove excess salt, taking care to keep the slices intact, then drain and dry the slices on clean tea towels.

Add the vinegar, sugar and spices to a large saucepan and bring to the boil. Add the tomatoes and bring to a gentle simmer, reduce the heat and cook for 2 minutes. Transfer to the sterilised preserving jars (see page 295). The pickled tomatoes will keep, unopened, for up to 12 months in a dark, dry place, and several months in the fridge once opened.

RONNIE:
CA'N PERE MUSSONA

Ca'n Pere Mussona, founded in 2006, is Ibiza's first certified organic livestock farm. It is dedicated to ethical animal rearing and promoting agricultural education and the preservation of rare and endangered Balearic Island breeds.

Ronnie Mussona, as he is known by the locals, is steeped in farming tradition. His wide-ranging interest in animal husbandry led him to work with the Association of the Black Pig of Formentera/Ibiza on a breeding programme backed by the University of Córdoba, which is dedicated to saving the critically endangered pig. In addition, Ca'n Pere Mussona is host to Mallorcan cows, as well as native breeds of chicken, sheep and rabbits, working to preserve the species in conjunction with Ibiza's indigenous breed associations.

Ca'n Pere Mussona is wonderful to visit: meticulously run, clean and green. The well-kept vegetable garden is full of native plant varieties, while surrounding fields produce organic livestock feed, making the farm self-sufficient. It is a model of sustainable, ethical farming and an exemplar of Ibiza's modern food movement.

Juniper gives its species name – *sabina* – to the traditional wooden roofing found in old houses and buildings across Ibiza. Sabina beams are a treasured feature of local architecture, and the juniper tree's fragrant berries are a beloved part of island cuisine. They pair exceptionally well with pork. To make the most of their flavour, toast the berries and crush them just before use. This makes enough for four people, with leftovers for the Pink Grapefruit and Juniper-Encrusted Pork Salad on page 58.

JUNIPER-ENCRUSTED PORK TENDERLOIN

Serves 4

❦ ❦ ❦ ❦ ❦ ❦ ❦ ❦ ❦ ❦ ❦

1kg (2lb 2oz) pork tenderloin, at room temperature
4 tbsp extra virgin olive oil, plus extra for massaging
2 tbsp whole juniper berries
2 tbsp coarse sea salt
1 tsp coarsely ground black pepper
75ml (3fl oz) white wine

Preheat the oven to 200°C (400°F), gas mark 6.

Trim off or tie under the narrow end of the tenderloin. Massage the meat with olive oil, shaping it into a log.

Toast the juniper berries in a hot, dry frying pan for 2–3 minutes, then crush them in a mortar and pestle.

Mix the crushed juniper berries, salt and pepper together and spread the mixture on a large plate. Dip both ends of the tenderloin in the salt mixture, then roll the tenderloin on the plate until it is completely coated in the spices. Press the mixture into the meat with your hands.

Heat the olive oil in a large, heavy-based frying pan until hot. Add the pork and let it sear for 3 minutes, then give it a quarter turn and sear for a further 3 minutes. Repeat until seared all over, then sear each end. Do not move the meat while it is searing: the seared bits will stick to the pan and be ripped off the meat.

Transfer the pork to a roasting tin and roast in the oven for 10–20 minutes, until a meat thermometer inserted into the pork reads 65°C (150°F). Remove the meat from the tin, transfer to a plate, cover loosely with foil and leave to rest for 10 minutes.

While the meat is resting, deglaze both the frying pan and the roasting tin with the white wine and pass the liquid through a sieve into a bowl or jug.

Cut three-quarters of the pork into 2cm (¾in) thick slices, place on plates and pour the pan liquid over the meat to serve.

Set aside the remaining pork for the Pink Grapefruit and Juniper-Encrusted Pork Salad (see page 58).

Juniper-encrusted pork combined with pink grapefruit makes
a unique and delicious salad. It is the perfect reason to cook
extra tenderloin – cook once for two meals.

PINK GRAPEFRUIT AND JUNIPER-ENCRUSTED PORK SALAD

Serves 2–3

✦ ✦ ✦ ✦ ✦ ✦ ✦ ✦ ✦ ✦ ✦ ✦

150g (5oz) red and green
   baby lettuces
50g (2oz) baby spinach
1 pink grapefruit, peeled and
   segmented, juice reserved
250g (9oz) Juniper-Encrusted
   Pork Tenderloin (see page 56),
   cut into 2cm (¾in) thick slices
Handful microgreens
Salt and black pepper

Dressing
3 tbsp extra virgin olive oil
1 tbsp reserved pink
   grapefruit juice
1 tsp aged red wine vinegar
Pinch cayenne pepper
Salt and black pepper

Combine all the dressing ingredients in a jar, seal and shake well. Set aside.

Put the lettuces and baby spinach in a bowl. Add ½ tablespoon of the dressing and toss well. Taste and add more dressing if desired, then season with salt and pepper. Put the dressed lettuce on a platter and scatter over the grapefruit segments and pork slices.

Drizzle with grapefruit juice and a bit more dressing and finish with a sprinkling of salt and pepper. Scatter with the microgreens and serve.

This rib recipe is an adaption from my friend and *Eivissa* crew member, chef Neil Allen – a grill-master extraordinaire. The fresh herbs impart a real Ibiza flavour. These ribs make frequent appearances at Can Riero farm dinners, and it is a much-requested recipe. Delicious served with the Calçots, Artichokes and Asparagus on page 62.

SLOW-ROASTED BARBECUE RIBS

Serves 6

❧ ❧ ❧ ❧ ❧ ❧ ❧ ❧ ❧ ❧ ❧ ❧

2 racks ribs (3–4kg/6lb 6oz–8lb 8oz)
Extra virgin olive oil, for coating
2 tbsp coriander seeds
2 tbsp black peppercorns
3 litres (5 pints) chicken stock
8 bay leaves
4 whole red chillies, halved lengthways and deseeded
4 onions, quartered
4 lemons, quartered
1 fennel bulb, with fronds attached, halved
8 thyme sprigs
8 rosemary sprigs
Salt and black pepper

Barbecue sauce
500ml (18fl oz) Roasted Tomato Sauce (see page 282)
75ml (3fl oz) apple cider, red wine or sherry vinegar
75g (3oz) brown sugar
2 tbsp tomato paste
1½ tbsp pimentón dulce (sweet paprika)
½ tbsp pimentón picante (hot paprika)
¼ tsp cayenne pepper
¼ tsp ground coriander
¼ tsp ground cumin
2 large pinches ground cinnamon
1 large pinch ground nutmeg
2 bay leaves
1 tsp salt
¼ tsp black pepper

Coat the ribs with olive oil and sprinkle them liberally with salt and pepper. Place each rack in a large roasting tin. Turn on the oven grill to its highest setting and grill the ribs for 5–6 minutes on each side to brown.

Meanwhile, toast the coriander seeds and peppercorns in a hot, dry frying pan for 1–2 minutes, until fragrant, then crush in a mortar and pestle.

Put the stock in a large saucepan with the coriander, pepper and bay leaves and bring to the boil. Meanwhile, remove the ribs from the tins. Divide the chillies, onions, lemons, fennel, thyme and rosemary between the two tins. Return the ribs to the roasting tins, meat side up. Pour over enough chicken stock to nearly submerge them. Cover the tins with foil and bake at 160°C (320°F), gas mark 3 for 3 hours. Check them every hour to ensure there is still liquid in the tins, topping up with water or white wine if necessary. Remove the racks from the oven when the meat is nearly falling off the bone.

To make the barbecue sauce, place all the ingredients for the sauce in a heavy-based saucepan. Bring to a simmer over a medium heat, then reduce the heat to low (you can use a flame tamer or heat diffuser for even slower cooking). Cook the sauce, uncovered, for 1–2 hours until the sauce is very thick and slightly browned.

Drain the ribs and brush with barbecue sauce, then barbecue or grill the ribs for 10–15 minutes to caramelise the sauce before serving.

Calçots, which are harvested in the very early spring, resemble spring onions in flavour but are fatter and longer. Catalans love them so much they have festivals called *calçotades* where they eat nothing but calçots. Eating a mess of spring onions (the nearest substitute available outside of Catalonia) does not a fiesta make. Serving them with asparagus and artichokes to accompany the ribs on page 61, however, makes for a festive meal in the spirit of the *calçotada*. Traditionally calçots are grilled and served whole with charred skin intact. There is a specific technique for eating them: grasp the green inner portion of the stalk top with one hand and pinch the charred bottom just above where the root meets the vegetable. Then, pull the green inner portion out of the charred skin. Dip the white bottom in sauce, tip your head back to avoid dripping sauce down your front, and bite it off where the white meets the green. Heaven.

CALÇOTS, ARTICHOKES AND ASPARAGUS

Serves 10

❧ ❧ ❧ ❧ ❧ ❧ ❧ ❧ ❧ ❧ ❧

15 small or 10 large globe artichokes
Extra virgin olive oil
2–3 tbsp lemon juice
2kg (4lb 4oz) whole calçots or large spring onions, roots trimmed
1.5kg (3lb 4oz) asparagus (about 40 spears)
Salt and black pepper

Preheat the oven to 200°C (400°F), gas mark 6. Slice off the stem and top third of the artichokes. Place each artichoke stem-side down on a large square of foil. Drizzle each with 1 tablespoon of olive oil, ½ teaspoon of lemon juice, 1 teaspoon of water and a sprinkle of salt. Work the salt and oil into the leaves with your fingers, opening them slightly. Wrap completely in the foil. Put the foil package containing the artichokes on a baking tray and bake for 1 hour 5 minutes– 1 hour 25 minutes. They are done when a skewer pierced through the artichokes meets little resistance. Remove from the oven and set aside, keeping them in their foil package.

Preheat a barbecue grill or griddle pan. Place the calçots or spring onions on the grill and cook for 20–25 minutes, turning them regularly with tongs, until charred all over. Remove and wrap in newspaper so that they continue to steam-cook for a further 20 minutes.

Lightly oil the asparagus spears and season with salt. Grill the spears for 6–8 minutes until the stems are lightly browned and the flesh is *al dente*.

Serve the vegetables on a platter with bowls of Maltaise, vinaigrette and Romesco sauce (pages 281 and 283) for dipping.

Legs of local Ibiza lamb are small and densely flavoured. This slow-roasting technique works for any size of lamb leg, if you adjust the time accordingly. The yoghurt marinade enhances the flavour and tenderises the meat. This dish is great with broad beans (see page 290) and a Picante Yoghurt Sauce (see page 282).

SLOW-ROASTED MARINATED LEG OF LAMB

Serves 6

❧ ❧ ❧ ❧ ❧ ❧ ❧ ❧ ❧ ❧ ❧

1 leg of lamb
350ml (12fl oz) white wine
240ml (8½fl oz) vegetable stock
1 tbsp whole black peppercorns
4 garlic cloves, bashed
2 sprigs thyme or rosemary
1 dried red or cayenne chilli
Baby Broad Beans with Cumin
  (see page 290), to serve
Picante Yoghurt Sauce
  (see page 282), to serve

Marinade
1 tsp ground cumin
1 tsp ground coriander
⅛ tsp cayenne pepper
240g (8½oz) yoghurt
  (preferably goat's
  milk yoghurt)
2 garlic cloves, crushed
Salt and black pepper

To make the marinade, toast the ground cumin, coriander and cayenne in a hot, small dry frying pan for 2 minutes or until fragrant. Combine the yoghurt and garlic with the toasted spices in a bowl and season with salt and pepper.

Rub the marinade onto the lamb, covering it entirely. Wrap the lamb in clingfilm and marinate in the fridge for 24–48 hours.

Remove the lamb from the fridge and allow it to come to room temperature before roasting.

Preheat the oven to 200°C (400°F), gas mark 6. Put the leg on a rack in a deep roasting tin and put it in the hot oven for 20 minutes to brown.

While the lamb browns, bring the wine and stock to the boil in a large saucepan. Add the peppercorns, garlic, thyme or rosemary and dried chilli, reduce the heat and simmer for 20 minutes to combine the flavours.

Remove the lamb from the oven and pour the hot liquid straight into the hot roasting tin. Reduce the oven temperature to 120°C (250°F), gas mark ½, and bake the lamb for 6–8 hours, depending on the size of the leg. Check it every couple of hours and add more stock if the pan is dry. Use a meat thermometer to determine the length of cooking time. Lamb is rare at 60°C, medium at 65–70°C and well done at 75°C. Alternatively, test it by prodding it with tongs. Rare meat is yielding to the touch, medium feels springy and well-done meat is firm.

Remove the lamb from the oven, cover loosely with foil and leave to rest for 30 minutes before serving with broad beans and yoghurt sauce.

❧ ❧ ❧

Tip: Save the leg bone, wrapped carefully, in the freezer. It will add a great deal of flavour to stews and soups; in particular it is integral to Lentils with Merguez (see page 242).

This is a Can Riero classic. I learned from my mother that roasting the courgette shells ahead sets their gorgeous green colour and cooks them through. The final roasting is quicker and means that the stuffing doesn't dry out, resulting in a juicy stuffed courgette.

STUFFED COURGETTES

Serves 4

❧ ❧ ❧ ❧ ❧ ❧ ❧ ❧ ❧ ❧ ❧ ❧

4 small courgettes (about 800g/1¾lb), halved lengthways, seeds scooped out
Extra virgin olive oil
Pimentón dulce (sweet paprika)
Salt and black pepper

Stuffing
¼ tsp ground allspice
⅛ tsp ground bay leaf
⅛ tsp ground fennel seeds
¼ tsp cayenne pepper
3 tbsp olive oil
250g (9oz) minced lamb
1 small onion, finely chopped
1 garlic clove, finely chopped
75ml (3fl oz) red wine
50g (2oz) Roasted Red Peppers (see page 274), finely chopped, plus 1 extra roasted pepper, cut into 16 strips lengthways
30g (1¼oz) toasted pine nuts
10 pitted Kalamata olives, finely chopped
1 tsp grated lemon zest
1 tsp lemon juice
Small handful mint, leaves chopped
Small handful flat-leaf parsley, leaves chopped
60 g (2½oz) soft goat's cheese
50g (2oz) breadcrumbs
40g (1½oz) Manchego curado or Pecorino cheese, grated
Salt and black pepper

Set one oven rack at the lowest height and another two-thirds of the way up. Preheat the oven to 200°C (400°F), gas mark 6, and put a baking tray in the oven to heat up. Brush the courgettes with olive oil and season with salt, pepper and pimentón dulce. Roast them cut side down on the preheated baking tray on the bottom rack in the oven for 8–10 minutes until the skin wrinkles and the flesh is slightly soft. Remove and set aside (and keep the oven on).

To make the stuffing, combine the allspice, bay leaf, ground fennel and cayenne and toast for 1 minute in a hot, dry frying pan until fragrant, then add 1 tablespoon of the olive oil and fry the spices for 1–2 minutes until fragrant. Add the minced lamb and fry for 6–8 minutes until slightly browned, then remove from the heat, transfer to a bowl and set aside.

Return the pan to the heat, add the remaining olive oil, onion and garlic and fry for 4–5 minutes, until soft and lightly browned. Transfer the onion and garlic to the bowl with the lamb and deglaze the pan with the red wine. Set the wine aside.

Add the roasted red peppers, pine nuts, olives, lemon zest and juice, mint and parsley to the lamb and mix to combine. Add the goat's cheese and stir together until the cheese melts, then add the breadcrumbs, 1 teaspoon of salt and 1 teaspoon of pepper. Mix well. If the stuffing is too dry add a little of the wine from deglazing the pan. If too wet, add more breadcrumbs.

Stuff the courgettes with equal amounts of the lamb stuffing and place on the baking tray. Cover the tray with foil and bake for 20 minutes. Remove the foil, sprinkle the courgettes with grated cheese, and decorate each with 2 strips of red pepper. Bake uncovered for 5–8 minutes, until the cheese is melted and golden. Serve hot or at room temperature.

❧ ❧ ❧

Tip: The courgettes and the stuffing can be prepared in advance, so this makes a great dinner party dish. Stuff and roast them just before serving.

Ibiza's small, tender squid can be delicious on their own. If pressed
for time, simply grill and serve with green sauce (see page 130); however,
stuffed squid is impressive. *Sobrasada*, a spicy Balearic sausage, is the
traditional ingredient for stuffing. Spinach and prawns are lighter variations.
Presented together, the trio makes a very special meal.

SOBRASADA-STUFFED SQUID

Serves 4

❦ ❦ ❦ ❦ ❦ ❦ ❦ ❦ ❦ ❦

500g (1lb 2oz) small whole
    squid (frozen or fresh)
3 tbsp extra virgin olive oil,
    plus extra for brushing
3 tsp anchovy paste, or
    6 anchovies in oil, drained
    and finely chopped
1½ onions, finely chopped
3 garlic cloves, finely chopped
300g (10½oz) *sobrasada* or other
    spicy pork sausage, broken
    into pieces
150g (6oz) breadcrumbs
6 Roasted Tomatoes (see
    page 275), finely chopped
½ tsp chilli flakes
Sherry vinegar (optional)
350g (12oz) Roasted Tomato
    Sauce (see page 282), to serve
Salt and pepper

If you are using frozen squid, place it in a bowl of cold
water and leave it to defrost. Wash the fresh or defrosted
squid thoroughly, cut off the tentacles, then remove the hard
'quill' from inside the bodies and the ink sacs. Peel away the
skin and membranes from the meat. Remove and discard
the heads, then finely chop the tentacles and set aside.

Heat the olive oil in a frying pan over a medium heat. Add
the anchovy paste or chopped anchovies, then add the onions
and garlic and fry for 5–6 minutes, until soft and slightly golden.
Add the *sobrasada* or sausage and fry for a further 5–6 minutes
until lightly browned, then add the breadcrumbs and squid
tentacles and fry for a further 1–2 minutes. Add the roasted
tomatoes and chilli flakes. Stir to combine and cook for
3–4 minutes to heat through. Add a dash of sherry vinegar if
needed to brighten the flavour and season with salt and pepper.
Hold the squid bodies like an ice-cream cone, spoon in the
stuffing and pack them tight. Close them with a toothpick.

Brush the outsides of the stuffed squid with olive oil. Cook
under a medium grill, or in a griddle pan, for 4–5 minutes, until
the squid is golden and the stuffing hot through, turning them
carefully to grill all sides. Serve with Roasted Tomato Sauce
for dipping.

Spinach-Stuffed Squid

❦ ❦ ❦ ❦ ❦ ❦ ❦ ❦ ❦ ❦ ❦

500g (1lb 2oz) small whole squid (frozen or fresh)
3 tbsp extra virgin olive oil, plus extra for brushing
1½ onions, finely chopped
3 garlic cloves, crushed
150g (6oz) breadcrumbs
1.5kg (3lb 4oz) spinach, cooked and chopped
180g (7½oz) toasted pine nuts
4 tbsp lemon juice
Grated zest of 1½ lemons
3 handfuls flat-leaf parsley, leaves chopped
350g (12oz) Roasted Tomato Sauce
    (see page 282), to serve
Salt and pepper

❦ ❦ ❦ ❦ ❦ ❦ ❦ ❦ ❦ ❦ ❦

Prepare the squid as on page 69.

Heat the olive oil in a frying pan over a medium heat then add the onions and garlic and fry for 5–6 minutes until soft and slightly golden. Add the breadcrumbs and fry for a further 2–3 minutes until golden, then add the squid tentacles and cook for 1–2 minutes until the flesh turns opaque. Add the spinach, pine nuts and lemon juice and cook for a further 2–3 minutes to combine. Remove from the heat, add the lemon zest and parsley, mix well to combine and season with salt and pepper.

Fill the squid with stuffing and cook as on page 69. Serve with Roasted Tomato Sauce for dipping.

Prawn-Stuffed Squid

❦ ❦ ❦ ❦ ❦ ❦ ❦ ❦ ❦ ❦ ❦

500g (1lb 2oz) small whole squid (frozen or fresh)
3 tbsp extra virgin olive oil, plus extra for brushing
6 shallots, finely chopped
3 garlic cloves, finely chopped
150g (6oz) breadcrumbs
360g (13½oz) cooked, shelled prawns
½ tsp red chilli flakes
3 tbsp lemon juice
Grated zest of 1 lemon
2 large handfuls coriander leaves, chopped
350g (12oz) Roasted Tomato Sauce
    (see page 282), to serve
Salt and pepper

❦ ❦ ❦ ❦ ❦ ❦ ❦ ❦ ❦ ❦ ❦

Prepare the squid as on page 69.

Heat the olive oil in a frying pan over a medium heat. Add the shallots and garlic and fry for 4–5 minutes until soft and slightly golden. Add the squid tentacles and fry for a further 2–3 minutes, until the flesh turns opaque, then add the breadcrumbs, prawns, chilli flakes, lemon juice and lemon zest. Cook for 3–4 minutes to heat through. Remove from the heat, add the coriander leaves, stir and season with salt and pepper.

Fill the squid with stuffing and cook as on page 69. Serve with Roasted Tomato Sauce for dipping.

Octopus can be wonderful: tender and subtly salty, like the smell of the Mediterranean in the spring. It is readily available cooked and frozen, which is ideal for this recipe. Freezing the octopus tenderises the flesh and buying it cooked means you avoid any of the beating and boiling of raw octopus recommended by some Mediterranean cooks. This salad is a play on a Spanish classic: boiled octopus and potatoes, served on wooden plates and eaten with toothpicks, but with added excitement from the fresh, zesty flavours of mint, orange and olives.

OCTOPUS WITH POTATOES, OLIVES, MINT AND ORANGE

Serves 4

½ sweet red onion,
    sliced paper thin
300g (11oz) small new
    potatoes, peeled
2 tbsp extra virgin olive oil
400g (14oz) cooked, frozen
    octopus tentacles, thawed
    in the fridge or in a large
    bowl of water
2 oranges, peeled and
    segmented, juice reserved
24 pitted black olives or
    Kalamata olives
Handful mint leaves
Salt and black pepper

Dressing
3 tbsp extra virgin olive oil
2 tbsp reserved orange juice
½ tsp sherry vinegar
Pinch cayenne pepper
Salt and black pepper

Place the onion slices in a bowl of ice-cold water and leave them to soak for 20 minutes, then drain and pat dry.

Fill a medium saucepan two-thirds full of water and bring to the boil. Add the potatoes and a couple of large pinches of salt. Reduce the heat and simmer for 10–15 minutes, until the potatoes are *al dente*, then drain and set aside to cool. When the potatoes are cool, cut them into thirds, toss them with the olive oil and season with salt and pepper.

Peel off the purple outer membrane of the octopus tentacles and cut them into medium-sized chunks.

To make the dressing, put all the ingredients in a bottle, seal and shake well to mix. Taste and correct the seasoning, adding more vinegar or orange juice if desired.

Arrange the octopus, potatoes, orange segments, onions and black olives on a platter. Drizzle liberally with the dressing and scatter with the mint leaves.

Wild samphire grows along the edges of Ibiza's salt flats in early spring and it is a real pleasure to forage in such a beautiful, historic location. We walk carefully along the verges of the salt pans, picking the green shoots. Samphire tastes like the sea smells, much like an oyster. It pairs beautifully with steamed mussels, adding a burst of colour.

STEAMED MUSSELS WITH SAMPHIRE

Serves 4

✦ ✦ ✦ ✦ ✦ ✦ ✦ ✦ ✦ ✦ ✦ ✦

1kg (2lb 2oz) mussels
3 tbsp extra virgin olive oil
1 onion, finely chopped
2 shallots, finely chopped
3 garlic cloves, finely chopped
2 sticks celery, cut into 1cm
  (½in) thick half moons
3 tbsp vermouth
2 tbsp crème fraîche
150g (5oz) samphire
Salt and black pepper

Start by preparing the mussels. Scrub the mussels one at a time under cold running water to remove any barnacles, seaweed and sand, and check each mussel is firmly closed. If one is not, pinch it shut. If it stays shut keep it, if not, discard it. To debeard the mussels look for the small seaweed-like thread about halfway down the shell. Wiggle it loose, pull it out and discard.

Heat the olive oil in a heavy-based saucepan with a fitted lid, over a high heat. Add the onion, shallots and garlic and cook for 3–4 minutes until softened, then add the celery and mussels and fry for 1–2 minutes. Add the vermouth and crème fraîche, shake well to combine, then add the samphire. Cover the pan tightly and cook the mussels for 5–6 minutes over a high heat, lifting the lid and stirring every 2 minutes, checking that there is enough liquid and that the mussel shells are opening.

Remove from the heat, discard any mussels that are still closed and serve immediately with crusty bread for mopping up the juices.

BEES AND
BEE KEEPING

Bees are an essential part of arable farm life and hives are a joy to have on the land. They play an important role in the cultivation of fruit and vegetables, pollinating the plants that fill our gardens, orchards and surrounding land. On a spring day, there is no more intoxicating sound than the buzz of bees tumbling from tomato plant to squash vine to apple tree.

The byproduct of this hard work is gorgeous liquid gold – honey. Our neighbour, Vicente, a beekeeper for many years, taught me the basics of the organic apiary. We clean hives with lemon juice and gather and burn wild herbs in the smoker. The fragrant smoke helps calm the bees while we run routine checks for pests, clean the hives or collect honey. This slow, steady work is incredibly rewarding: both caring for the bees and gathering their delicious honey.

To appreciate its sweetness and subtle flavours, use wild honey with just one or two simple ingredients. On Ibiza local honey is traditionally paired with local fresh cheeses or yoghurt and a sprinkle of walnuts.

The beauty of this is that once you have the curd, dessert is ready in minutes. We use incredibly sweet organic strawberries from local grower Agroturismo, Can Martí. If you're fortunate to have equally delicious fruit, reduce the sugar. Try the other curds too: both lemon and grapefruit are great with strawberries (see pages 287–88).

STRAWBERRY AND BLOOD ORANGE CURD PARFAIT

Serves 4

❦ ❦ ❦ ❦ ❦ ❦ ❦ ❦ ❦ ❦ ❦

300g (11oz) fresh strawberries,
  hulled and thickly sliced
3 tbsp caster sugar, or to taste
1 tbsp Grand Marnier
1 x quantity Stabilised Whipped
  Cream (see page 286)
1 x quantity Blood Orange Curd
  (see page 288)

Mix the sliced strawberries in a bowl with the sugar and Grand Marnier. Leave to macerate at room temperature for 15–20 minutes, until the strawberries begin to give up their juice.

Layer the cream, curd and strawberries in a large glass bowl, or individual glasses or dishes, and serve immediately.

❦ ❦ ❦

Tip: You can prepare the curd ahead of time and, 15 minutes before serving, make the Stabilised Whipped Cream and assemble.

The flavour of this cake is about as intense as grapefruit gets. The sweet, moist sponge plays well against the tartness of the grapefruit curd. Topped with candied grapefruit it is fabulous and really quite beautiful.

PINK GRAPEFRUIT CAKE WITH CURD AND CANDIED GRAPEFRUIT

Serves 8–10

❦ ❦ ❦ ❦ ❦ ❦ ❦ ❦ ❦ ❦ ❦

You will need: 23cm (9in) round springform cake tin

Cake
200g (7oz) unsalted butter, softened, plus extra for greasing
225g (8oz) self-raising flour, sifted, plus extra for dusting
225g (8oz) caster sugar
Finely grated zest of ½ grapefruit
2 tbsp pink grapefruit juice
4 eggs, at room temperature
225g (8oz) self-raising flour, sifted, plus extra for dusting
50g (2oz) plain Greek yoghurt
1 x quantity Pink Grapefruit Curd (see page 288)

Candied grapefruit
150g (5oz) caster sugar
1 grapefruit, cut into ½cm (¼in) thick rounds

Preheat the oven to 180°C (350°F), gas mark 4. Grease the base and sides of the cake tin with butter and dust with flour. Line the base with baking parchment and grease the parchment.

Cream together the butter, sugar, grapefruit zest and juice in the bowl of a stand mixer at medium-high speed until pale, light and fluffy, or in a mixing bowl with a hand-held electric whisk. The sugar should be worked in, leaving a slightly grainy texture. Add the eggs, one at a time, beating well after each addition. Fold in the flour and yoghurt in three stages, taking care not to knock out too much of the air from the batter. The batter should slide easily off a spoon: if it is too thick add more yoghurt.

Pour the batter into the prepared tin and level the top with a spatula. Pick up the pan and knock the base on the work surface to get rid of any air bubbles. Bake for 40–50 minutes until golden brown, risen and springy to the touch – a toothpick inserted into the middle of it should come out clean. Remove from the oven and cool it in the tin for 15 minutes, then remove it from the tin and leave to cool completely on a wire rack.

To make the candied grapefruit, bring 150ml (5fl oz) of water to the boil in a large frying pan. Add the sugar and stir until completely dissolved, then cover the bottom of the pan with a single layer of grapefruit slices. Reduce the heat and simmer for 6–8 minutes until the grapefruit is translucent. Transfer the fruit to a plate lined with baking parchment and repeat with the remaining slices. Cool at room temperature.

Slice the cooled cake in half horizontally through the middle and fill it with grapefruit curd. Top with the candied grapefruit.

Caramelised grapefruit and Campari is a fabulous retro combination: crisp, sweet and tart. The sound of the spoon shattering the caramelised sugar is pure anticipation. Pink grapefruit and Campari also make the perfect spring cocktail: grapefruit juice, Campari, soda water and Grand Marnier is a Can Riero Easter brunch classic.

CARAMELISED GRAPEFRUIT HALVES WITH CAMPARI

Serves 4

2 pink grapefruits
4 tbsp Campari
4 tbsp caster sugar

Turn the oven grill to its highest setting and place the oven rack directly beneath the grill.

Cut the grapefruits in half horizontally. Use a sharp paring knife to cut the flesh away from the inside of the peel and white membrane. Cut along the inside of each membrane, against the flesh, to separate the segments, cutting to the bottom without piercing the peel. The segments should be easy to prise from the shell when cooked.

Place the grapefruit halves on a baking tray and poke the top of the grapefruit segments with a toothpick. Drizzle 1 tablespoon of Campari over each half and set aside for 10 minutes to allow it to soak into the fruit. Sprinkle each half with 1 tablespoon of sugar, completely coating the tops of the grapefruits, and immediately place them under the grill. Grill the grapefruit halves for 2 minutes, then turn the tray or move the fruits if necessary to ensure they caramelise evenly. Grill for a further 1–2 minutes, until the sugar is completely caramelised. Serve straight away.

Pitting, stuffing and dipping the cherries is a bit more work than
the average after-dinner chocolate, but these truffles are well worth it.
They are absolutely, cannot-stop-eating scrumptious. Make extra:
they will be wholeheartedly consumed.

TRUFFLED CHOCOLATE CHERRIES

Makes about 300g (11oz)

200g (7oz) ripe cherries
50ml (2fl oz) double cream
Tiny pinch ground cinnamon
200g (7oz) dark chocolate,
    roughly chopped
1 tbsp cherry liqueur

Pit the cherries with a cherry pitter, pitting from the side in
order to leave the stem intact. Set aside.

Bring the cream and cinnamon to the boil in a small saucepan.

Put half the chopped chocolate in a heatproof bowl. Pour in
the hot cream and set aside to melt.

Once the chocolate has melted, mix the cherry liqueur into
the cream and chocolate and allow the mixture to cool to room
temperature, then chill. It will thicken as it cools.

Fit a piping bag with a small nozzle and spoon the cooled
chocolate mixture into the bag. Fill the cherries with the truffle
mixture, taking care not to overfill them.

Line a baking tray with baking parchment. Put the remaining
chocolate in a heatproof bowl and place the bowl over a
saucepan of barely simmering water, making sure the bottom
of the bowl doesn't touch the water. Once the chocolate has
melted, remove the bowl from the pan. Dip the stuffed cherries
in the melted chocolate, holding the stems and fully immersing
them, then lay them on the lined baking tray. Transfer to the
fridge to set.

SUMMER

The Ibiza summer, with its cloudless, intensely blue skies and hot Mediterranean sun, begins with the ripening of glorious fruit. Apricots, cherries, peaches, plums, mulberries and strawberries all come in quick succession, perfectly ripe and sun-kissed, sweet and dripping juice, so much so that they need to be picked with a tender hand. They are often warm to the touch and fragrant, and offer a riot of colour – gorgeous yellows, purples, oranges and reds. We keep bowls full of these luscious fruits for every whim – eating out of hand, using in granitas, in purées for the freezer, as fruit salads for breakfast, or to accompany a biscuit and some cream for dessert. They are the taste of the early summer sun.

Some time around the beginning of July the sun goes from hot to scorching; suddenly the lush green vegetables and herbs of the long spring and early summer give way to fruit of another sort: our heirloom tomatoes, one of the great joys of the season. Mid-morning, when the sun has hit the vines sufficiently, the field is an intoxicating place to be, the pungent scent of the vines interplanted with basil and the sweet, slightly acidic flavour of the sun-warmed tomatoes is one of the many pleasures of Can Riero. Peppers follow – red, green, yellow and orange, sweet and hot varieties, then aubergine a bit later on; all three evocative of true Mediterranean flavours.

We plant aubergine later than the heirlooms, in mid-spring, along with our sauce tomatoes, preferring to have them ready when it's time to return to the kitchen. Our aubergines and peppers will go on the grill at night – even the tomatoes – along with meat and chicken. The Ibiza classic of grilled fish, local potatoes and aioli are beach-restaurant staples, but very little cooking with heat happens in the Can Riero kitchen, particularly during the day. Our food is cool: chilled soups, fresh salads, small bites and shared plates – all a riot of flavours.

Can Riero's long, scorching August days are, in their own way, similar to winter; it is a time of dying back. The unvarying cloudless skies and fierce Mediterranean sun send all but the hardiest plants into retreat. Ibiza's *campo*, far from being the lush green of spring, takes on gold, soft-burnt hues, except for the pines which linger and add a dash of green. Hot and arid ripples are visible; the earth is truly parched.

In Spain, gazpacho is a very personal thing. There seem to be as many recipes as there are cooks and everyone is passionate about how they make it. It's best to keep it simple, using vegetables that are picked and prepared the same day. The idea of adding melon comes from Paula Wolfert, the doyenne of Mediterranean cooking. The melon's sweetness softens the acidity and helps lift the flavour of regular tomatoes.

GAZPACHO

Serves 6, with leftovers

❧ ❧ ❧ ❧ ❧ ❧ ❧ ❧ ❧ ❧ ❧

1kg (2lb 2oz) ripe tomatoes, peeled and deseeded
2 small cucumbers, peeled
½ red pepper, deseeded
1 sweet onion, peeled
300g (11oz) ripe, white-fleshed melon, peeled and deseeded
2 garlic cloves, crushed
1 tsp salt
Pinch cumin seeds
Pinch coriander seeds
2 tbsp extra virgin olive oil, plus extra for drizzling
1 tsp sherry vinegar
Salt and black pepper
1 ripe avocado, to serve
Chopped chives, to serve

Roughly chop the vegetables and melon. Combine them in a bowl with the garlic, add the salt and mix, then chill for 2–3 hours, to allow the flavours to marry and the vegetables and melon to release their juices.

Meanwhile, toast the cumin and coriander seeds in a hot, dry frying pan for 1–2 minutes, until fragrant, then crush them in a mortar and pestle.

Purée the vegetables with a hand-held blender, then add the oil, vinegar, ground cumin and coriander and blend again until completely incorporated. Season to taste and chill for 1 hour, or until ready to serve.

Stone, peel and chop the avocado. Garnish the soup with chopped avocado, chives and a drizzle of olive oil.

❧ ❧ ❧

Tip: For a casual meal, purée the soup to a rustic coarse texture. For a more elegant finish, purée until smooth, pass it through a food mill then serve it with fried cubes of bread and finely chopped, peeled and deseeded cucumber.

Watermelon is a summer staple on Ibiza. It is everywhere: in shops, market stalls, vegetable stands as well as decorating green vines in the fields. Sweet, crisp and juicy, it is serious refreshment when combined with the salty, sour and spicy flavours of this soup. Always eat this very cold: it is pure re-energizing hydration when the summer heat is at its peak. To eat it at its best, prepare it in the morning to serve in the evening, giving the flavours time to combine.

WATERMELON GAZPACHO

Serves 6

❧ ❧ ❧ ❧ ❧ ❧ ❧ ❧ ❧ ❧ ❧

1kg (2lb 2oz) watermelon
    flesh, chopped
1 large tomato, peeled
    and deseeded
1 large cucumber, peeled
    and chopped
¼ sweet onion, chopped
½ red pepper, chopped
1–2 fresh red chillies,
    deseeded and chopped
4 tbsp extra virgin olive oil
Juice and finely grated zest
    of 2 limes
2 tsp agave syrup (optional)
Salt and black pepper

To serve
350g (12oz) watermelon flesh,
    roughly chopped
1 small cucumber, chopped
1 large yellow or green
    tomato, chopped
¼ red onion, very thinly sliced
75g (3oz) feta cheese
Handful mint, leaves sliced
    into ribbons
Salt and black pepper

First make the soup base. Purée the watermelon, tomato, cucumber, onion, red pepper, 1 chilli, olive oil, a large pinch of lime zest and 3 tablespoons of the juice in a bowl or jug with a hand-held blender, or in the bowl of a food processor until smooth. Taste and add more lime juice, chilli and/or agave syrup. Season to taste and chill until ready to serve.

Divide the chopped vegetables among the serving bowls then spoon over the chilled soup base.

Garnish each serving with crumbled feta, mint ribbons, salt, pepper and a pinch of lime zest.

MAHÓN CHEESE

A Mahón cheese curing room is a symphony of fabulous scents: deep tones of wood, mushroom and yeast; the high sharp note of buttermilk; rich harmonies of sweet hay and ripe berries. The colours of the rinds range from pale gold, apricot and deep orange to lichen grey and smoky charcoal.

Menorca's cheese-making heritage stretches back over 1500 years. When the British colonised the island in the the 1700s they imported Friesians, and local cheesemakers used these new higher-producing dairy cattle to perfect a distinctive cow's milk cheese: Mahón. The second Spanish cheese (after Manchego) to earn PDO (Protected Designation of Origin) status, Mahón is recognisable for its square-pillow-with-rounded-corners shape. Two legal designations govern production: 'Artesà' cheese is made on farms using milk from their own cows – pasturised or raw. Plain 'Mahón' is made from raw (*crudo*) or pasturised milk purchased from local farms.

Every block of Mahón is stamped with two numbers: one for the farm (*finca*) where it was made, the other for its week of production. Age defines its characteristics and classifications: Semi-curado (aged 2-5 months) is mellow-tasting with a slight tang, with a consistency similar to medium Cheddar: smooth and dense. It has a velvety soft texture and melts beautifully, which makes it great for *gratinados*, *bocadillos*, burgers, eggs and in pasta dishes. Curado, cured for 6-12 months, develops a fabulous nutty flavour and crystalline texture similar to Parmesan. You can use this as a substitute for Parmesan or Pecorino, or it is equally good eaten alone. Most delicious (and almost impossible to find outside the island) is añejo. Cured for one year or more, añejo is fine-grained with concentrated notes of mushrooms, berries and sour curd. Like Bellota ham, Mahón añejo should be served simply with fabulous bread and olive oil.

These small bites are best made at the height of peach season, which on Ibiza is early summer. The combination of sweet juicy peach, rich salty ham and nutty and sharp Mahón crisps makes for a magnificent bite. They are sublime served with a glass of chilled Cava or a rich Spanish white wine.

PEACH AND SERRANO HAM WITH MAHÓN CRACKERS

Makes 20 crackers

❧ ❧ ❧ ❧ ❧ ❧ ❧ ❧ ❧ ❧

160g (5½oz) Mahón curado, Parmesan or extra-mature Cheddar cheese
100g (3½oz) thinly sliced Serrano ham
2 ripe peaches, cut into 20 thin wedges
20 mint leaves

Preheat the oven to 160°C (320°F), gas mark 3, and line a baking tray with baking parchment. Use a narrow glass or a 6cm (2½in) round biscuit cutter as a guide and draw 20 circles on the paper.

Coarsely grate the cheese. Fill each circle with a generous pinch of the cheese and bake in the oven for 12–15 minutes, until the cheese is melted, golden and crisp. Remove and set aside to cool completely.

Arrange a slice of ham, a piece of peach and a mint leaf on each cheese crisp and serve immediately.

This is the salad to make on Ibiza's dog day afternoons. Simple, fast, it is a real refresher: cool, sweet, salty and slightly acidic all at once – perfect.

WATERMELON AND TOMATO SALAD WITH GOAT'S CHEESE

Serves 4

❧ ❧ ❧ ❧ ❧ ❧ ❧ ❧ ❧ ❧ ❧

½ red onion, sliced paper thin
500g (1lb 2oz) watermelon
    flesh, cut into chunks
4 tomatoes (a combination of
    red, green, orange and yellow),
    cut into eighths
60g (2½oz) pitted black olives
Handful basil leaves, cut
    into ribbons
120g (4½oz) soft goat's cheese
Extra virgin olive oil,
    for drizzling
Dash aged sherry vinegar,
    to serve
Salt and black pepper

Place the onion slices in a bowl of ice-cold water and leave them to soak for 15 minutes. Drain, then pat dry with kitchen paper.

Toss together the fruit, olives and basil. Crumble the goat's cheese over the top, drizzle with olive oil, a dash of aged sherry vinegar and season to taste.

This recipe illustrates the fundamental culinary truth that a good dish is the sum of well-flavoured components and perfectly constructed bites. Fork up some mixed leaves and crab, dip them in the creamy sauce, then add a dot of hot sauce. Exquisite.

CRAB SALAD WITH CAPER CREAM AND HOT SAUCE

Serves 4

❧ ❧ ❧ ❧ ❧ ❧ ❧ ❧ ❧ ❧ ❧

150g (5oz) mixed lettuce leaves
1–2 tbsp extra virgin olive oil
300g (11oz) cooked fresh white
    crab meat (or good-quality
    tinned white crab meat)
1 lemon, cut into 4 wedges
Salt and black pepper
4 tsp Habanero Hot Sauce
    (see page 284), to serve

Caper cream
3 tbsp large capers, plus
    a splash of the caper brine
4 tbsp plain yoghurt
4 tbsp crème fraîche
Grated zest of ½ lemon

Lightly dress the greens in a bowl with the olive oil, season with salt and pepper and set aside.

To make the caper cream, finely chop 2 tablespoons of the capers. In a small bowl combine the yoghurt, crème fraîche, chopped capers, caper brine and lemon zest. Stir to combine and season with salt and pepper.

Arrange a handful of dressed leaves on each plate and top with a quarter of the crab meat. Squeeze a lemon wedge over the crab and sprinkle black pepper over the top. Serve the hot sauce and caper cream in individual bowls, or add 1 tablespoon of each to each plate, and garnish the salad with the remaining whole capers.

Don't mix the sauces. Distinct flavours are the secret to the perfect bite.

Simmering the poaching liquid with the herbs and aromatics is well worth the extra 30 minutes' wait, as the prawns take on the flavour of the seasoning in the liquid, giving far more depth to the dish. The prawns are also great served as a shared plate with Bravas sauce (see recipe page 293).

PRAWN AND SERRANO HAM SALAD

Serves 4

✤ ✤ ✤ ✤ ✤ ✤ ✤ ✤ ✤ ✤ ✤

80g (3¼oz) cherry tomatoes, quartered
Large handful basil, leaves torn
½ tsp salt
600g (1¼lb) shelled prawns, digestive tract removed
65g (2¾oz) yoghurt
65g (2¾oz) crème fraîche
4 drops Habanero Hot Sauce (see page 284)
¼ tsp freshly ground black pepper
2 tbsp extra virgin olive oil
75g (3oz) sliced Serrano ham
100g (3½oz) rocket
1 ripe avocado, stoned, peeled and sliced
Small bunch chives, snipped
Salt and black pepper

Poaching liquid
1 onion, quartered
1 lemon, sliced
6 garlic cloves, crushed
1 tbsp black peppercorns
4 bay leaves
2 whole fresh red chillies
1 tsp coriander seeds
750ml (25fl oz) water

To make the poaching liquid, tie the aromatics into a muslin making a little bundle. Put the bundle in a large saucepan with the water and bring to the boil. Reduce the heat and simmer, uncovered, for 30 minutes.

Meanwhile, combine the cherry tomatoes, most of the basil (reserving some to garnish) and salt in a bowl and set aside for 20 minutes.

Add the prawns to the poaching liquid and cook for 2–3 minutes, until just opaque. Strain through a sieve and set the prawns aside.

Make a dressing by mixing together the yoghurt, crème fraîche, hot sauce and black pepper in a bowl, then add the prawns.

Heat half of the olive oil in a frying pan until very hot, then add the sliced ham and fry for 1–2 minutes, until slightly crispy. Remove from the heat and transfer to a plate lined with kitchen paper, to drain.

Toss the rocket with the remaining olive oil, and season with salt and pepper.

To serve, place some dressed rocket on each plate then top with the prawns, add the cherry tomatoes and divide the avocado and crispy Serrano onto each plate. Sprinkle with the chives and remaining basil ribbons.

✤ ✤ ✤

Tip: Really do simmer the prawns for only a couple of minutes, then remove from the heat immediately when they become opaque and slightly underdone. They will continue to cook as they cool.

On Ibiza and across Spain, salads are typically served undressed, with olive oil, vinegar and salt and pepper brought to the table instead. Dressing salads at the table makes complete sense: each plate gets the perfect balance of acidity and oil according to personal taste. The method works well for this salad in particular because it preserves the delicious crunch of the dried bread.

IBICENCO TOMATO BREAD SALAD

Serves 4

❧ ❧ ❧ ❧ ❧ ❧ ❧ ❧ ❧ ❧ ❧

1 small sweet onion, cut into paper-thin slices
750g (1lb 10oz) tomatoes, preferably mixed red, orange, yellow and green
300g (11oz) Pita Bread (see page 292) or sliced ciabatta, oven-dried and coarsely crumbled
50g (2oz) pitted black olives
Small handful basil leaves
Small handful coriander leaves
125g (4½oz) Manchego curado or Pecorino cheese, shaved
Extra virgin olive oil
Good-quality red wine vinegar
Salt and black pepper

Place the onion slices in a bowl of ice-cold water and leave to soak for 20 minutes, then drain and pat dry with kitchen paper.

Cut the tomatoes into chunks – first cut into eight wedges then cut the wedges in half – and tip them into a bowl. Salt them liberally and leave them to sit for 20 minutes.

Add the crumbled bread, onion slices, olives, herbs and cheese to the tomatoes and toss well. Serve immediately with olive oil, red wine vinegar, salt and pepper for individual dressing.

This is a simple yet perfect method for serving vine-ripened tomatoes.
We usually avoid using the oven in the hottest months but we do make
an exception for this quick, delicious summer evening meal.

TOMATO GRATINADO

Serves 6

❦ ❦ ❦ ❦ ❦ ❦ ❦ ❦ ❦ ❦ ❦

1kg (2lb 2oz) tomatoes, cut
    into 2cm (¾in) thick slices
1 large bunch basil, leaves cut
    into ribbons
2 tbsp sherry vinegar, or to taste
½ ciabatta, sliced, fried and
    crumbled
50g (2oz) Mahón curado or
    Parmesan cheese, grated
30g (1¼oz) toasted walnuts,
    roughly chopped
Extra virgin olive oil
Salt and black pepper

Preheat the oven to 175°C (350°F), gas mark 4.

Place the tomato slices in a bowl, sprinkle with salt and set aside for 10 minutes.

Grease a glass or ceramic baking dish with oil, and cover the bottom with a layer of tomatoes. Scatter some of the ribboned basil leaves over the top. Season with salt, pepper and a sprinkle of sherry vinegar. Continue layering until all the tomatoes and basil are used up.

In a separate bowl, combine the crumbled ciabatta and grated cheese and season with salt and pepper.

Sprinkle the crumble mixture over the tomatoes then transfer to the oven and bake for 20 minutes. Remove from the oven and sprinkle over the walnuts. Increase the oven temperature to 200°C (400°F), gas mark 6 and bake the *gratinado* for a further 3–4 minutes until crisp.

Hands down, my family's favourite summer pasta. What makes it different is salting the tomatoes ahead, it's transformative. Combined with basil, chives and mozzarella, simple Mediterranean flavours don't get better than this.

TOMATO PASTA

Serves 4

❧ ❧ ❧ ❧ ❧ ❧ ❧ ❧ ❧ ❧ ❧

500g (1lb 2oz) tomatoes,
   preferably mixed colours,
   roughly chopped
500g (1lb 2oz) penne pasta
80ml (3fl oz) extra virgin olive oil
Large bunch basil, leaves torn
Large bunch chives, snipped
500g (1lb 2oz) mozzarella
   (about 2 large balls)
Salt and black pepper

Put the tomatoes in a salad bowl and sprinkle with two large pinches of salt. Set aside for 20 minutes.

Cook the pasta according to the packet instructions, then drain it and add to the tomatoes. Drizzle over the olive oil and the herbs.

Tear the mozzarella into pieces, add to the bowl with tomatoes and pasta. Toss thoroughly to coat with the oil and herbs. Season with salt and pepper before serving.

'Spatchcocked' chicken is a whole bird with the backbone removed so it can be flattened to cook. This makes for faster cooking, evenly moist flesh and crispy skin. This version, marinated with lovely Mediterranean herbs and glazed with brandy, makes a delicious summer dinner.

BRANDY-GLAZED GRILLED SPATCHCOCKED CHICKEN

Serves 4

❧ ❧ ❧ ❧ ❧ ❧ ❧ ❧ ❧ ❧ ❧

80ml (3fl oz) extra virgin olive oil
3 tbsp balsamic vinegar
Large handful thyme sprigs
4 sprigs rosemary
4 whole fresh cayenne or jalapeño chillies, de-stemmed and halved lengthways
6 garlic cloves, crushed
6 pared strips of lemon peel
1 free-range organic chicken, backbone removed
Salt and black pepper

Basting glaze
100ml (3½fl oz) brandy
50g (2oz) unsalted butter
2 tbsp soft light brown sugar

❧ ❧ ❧

Tip: Cook the chicken to nearly done before adding the glaze to prevent the glaze from burning; the glaze is a last-minute crisper.

Put the oil, vinegar, herbs, chillies, garlic and lemon peel in a resealable freezer bag, seal and shake to combine.

Season the chicken liberally with salt and pepper then place it in the bag. Seal and massage the meat in the bag to completely coat it in the oil mixture. Leave to marinate in the fridge for 24 hours.

Remove the chicken from the fridge and let it reach room temperature before cooking.

Preheat a barbecue grill or griddle pan until hot. Place the marinated chicken on the grill, skin-side down, for 10 minutes. Leave the lid open if barbecuing and do not move the chicken while it's cooking.

Meanwhile, combine the ingredients for the brandy glaze in a small saucepan and heat until it bubbles.

Turn the chicken over, baste the skin with brandy glaze, and grill for a further 10 minutes. Turn it over again so it is skin-side down, baste the flesh liberally with more glaze and cook for a further 10 minutes. Turn, baste the skin and grill for another 10 minutes. Turn over again, baste the skin generously and place skin-side down on the hottest part of the grill for another 5–8 minutes to finish. The chicken should be thoroughly browned and come away easily from the grill.

Insert a meat thermometer into the thickest part of the chicken to check that the meat has reached a safe temperature of 74°C (165°F), or transfer it to the oven to finish cooking if you are unsure whether it's cooked through.

Slow-roasting takes time but the prep is quick and the result is delicious, moist, falling-off-the-bone pork. Don't skip the garlic slivers, they add immense flavour.

SUMMER SLOW-ROASTED PORK SHOULDER WITH FENNEL AND LEMON

Serves 10 (with leftovers for the Lomo Cuban Bocadillo)

❦ ❦ ❦ ❦ ❦ ❦ ❦ ❦ ❦ ❦ ❦

1 tsp whole black peppercorns
1 tsp fennel seeds
2kg (4lb 4oz) Boston butt
    or pork shoulder, de-boned
5 garlic cloves, sliced into slivers
Extra virgin olive oil
750ml (25fl oz) chicken stock
175ml (6fl oz) vermouth
1 large onion, sliced
1 fennel bulb, fronds removed,
    sliced
Peel of 1 lemon, pared in strips
    with a carrot peeler
Handful fresh thyme
2 fresh cayenne or jalapeño
    chillies, halved lengthways
Salt and black pepper

❦ ❦ ❦

Tip: The pork tastes even better when made a day in advance.

Preheat the oven to 220°C (430°F), gas mark 7, and toast the peppercorns and fennel seeds in a dry frying pan until fragrant. Remove from the heat.

Using the tip of a paring knife, cut small slits into the pork, all over (top and bottom). Insert the garlic slivers, pushing them deep into the cuts. Massage the pork with plenty of olive oil, salt and pepper.

Transfer the pork to a roasting tin and roast in the oven for 15–20 minutes, until browned, then reduce the heat to 130°C (265°F), gas mark 1.

Meanwhile, bring the stock and vermouth to the boil in a saucepan.

Remove the pork from the oven and take it out of the roasting tin. Add the onion, fennel, stock and vermouth, lemon peel, thyme, toasted peppercorns and fennel seeds and chillies to the tin. Place a rack in the tin, place the pork on the rack, cover the tin with foil and bake in the oven for 8 hours, basting the pork every 3–4 hours, and turning up the heat for a few minutes each time you open the oven door to bring it back up to temperature.

Once the pork has been cooking for 8 hours, remove it from the oven and set it aside to rest. Press the vegetables in the tin to expel any juice and pass the tin liquid through a sieve. Chill the liquid for 2 hours or overnight then skim off the layer of fat at the top.

Meanwhile, shred the pork using two forks, discarding any large lumps of fat but incorporating any small bits. Set aside.

Put the skimmed cooking liquid in a saucepan, bring it to the boil, then simmer until reduced by half. Season with salt and pepper then pour the liquid over the shredded pork and combine to serve.

Freshly-made *bocadillos* (sandwiches) are a staple of Spanish cuisine. This Cuban-inspired *bocadillo* is a fabulous way to use leftover Slow-Roasted Pork Shoulder (see opposite). It makes a day-after lunch every bit as delicious as the previous night's dinner.

LOMO CUBAN BOCADILLO

Serves 3–4

❦ ❦ ❦ ❦ ❦ ❦ ❦ ❦ ❦ ❦ ❦

1 ciabatta or rustic baguette, halved lengthways
Extra virgin olive oil
100g (3½oz) smoked Serrano ham
500g (1lb 2oz) Slow-Roasted Pork, plus cooking liquid (see page 114)
100g (3½oz) Manchego semi-curado or Gouda cheese, thinly sliced
40g (1½oz) Cucumber and Onion Pickles (see page 277)

Dressing
3 tbsp extra virgin olive oil
1 tsp crème fraîche
½ tsp soft light brown sugar
1½ tsp lemon juice

Slaw
1 fennel bulb, trimmed and thinly sliced
½ kohlrabi bulb, peeled, sliced and cut lengthways into batons
¼ red onion, very thinly sliced
2 carrots, grated
100g (3½oz) cooked black beans
¼ tsp fennel seeds, toasted and ground in a mortar and pestle
Handful flat-leaf parsley leaves
Salt and black pepper

Brush both cut sides of the bread liberally with olive oil. Heat more olive oil in a frying pan and fry the ham for 2–3 minutes. Set aside on a plate lined with kitchen paper.

Shred the pork and moisten it with 1–2 tablespoons of its cooking liquid. Layer the pork, crispy Serrano ham and cheese on the bottom half of the bread. Put both bread halves under a hot grill for 3–4 minutes until the cheese has melted and the bread is lightly toasted.

Meanwhile, put all the ingredients for the dressing in a small jar. Seal and shake well. Combine all the vegetables for the slaw and toss with the dressing. Season with salt and pepper.

Remove the bread from the grill and top it with a generous spoonful of slaw and a few pickles.

Slice the sandwich into 3–4 pieces and serve immediately.

Skirt steak is a staple of the barbecues at my friend Vicente's horse stable. It is grilled on a makeshift grate over an open fire beneath the navy blue Ibiza evening sky. Simply prepared and quickly seared, the steaks are then sliced up on an old board, passed around and eaten straight out of the hand, or from the tip of a knife. I serve it with spicy chimichurri, smoky grilled vegetables (see page 291) and griddled flatbread.

MARINATED ENTRAÑA WITH CHIMICHURRI

Serves 6

❦ ❦ ❦ ❦ ❦ ❦ ❦ ❦ ❦ ❦ ❦

1.5kg (3lb 4oz) skirt steak, cut into strips

Marinade
120ml (4½fl oz) extra virgin olive oil
3 tbsp sherry vinegar
6 garlic cloves, crushed
1 fresh red chilli, deseeded and chopped
Grated zest of 1 lemon
Large handful rosemary leaves
Large handful thyme leaves
Salt and black pepper

Chimichurri
240ml (8½fl oz) extra virgin olive oil
90ml (3½fl oz) red wine vinegar
Large handful flat-leaf parsley, leaves roughly chopped
Handful oregano, leaves roughly chopped
Handful coriander, leaves roughly chopped
1 dried red chilli, deseeded and finely chopped
4 garlic cloves, finely chopped

To make the marinade, combine the oil, vinegar, garlic, chilli, lemon zest and herbs in a measuring jug and mix well.

Divide the strips of skirt steak into three large resealable freezer bags and pour a third of the marinade into each. Seal and massage the meat in the bag, to completely coat it. Transfer to the fridge to marinate for 24 hours.

Remove the steak strips from the fridge 30 minutes before cooking and preheat the barbecue or a griddle pan to very hot. Remove the steak from the marinade, reserving 4 tablespoons of the marinade for the grilled vegetables (see page 291).

Place all the ingredients for the chimichurri in a jar, seal it and shake well to combine. Set aside until needed.

Season the steak strips with salt and pepper and grill them on the grill or griddle pan for 3 minutes on each side for medium-rare, or 4 minutes for medium-well done – any longer and the steak will be tough as it is a very thin cut. Remove the steak from the grill and leave to rest for 5 minutes, then slice on the diagonal and serve with grilled vegetables (see page 291), chimichurri and some flatbread.

Grill aficionado Tom Mollo shared the gaucho juice secret with us.
He learned it from an Argentine grill master – hence the term 'gaucho juice'.
Legend has it that Argentine cowboys carried a version of this sauce in their
saddlebags. It is fantastic on any cut of meat; it eliminates the need for
a marinade and the salt enlivens the flavour. On a well-hung
sirloin it is nothing short of miraculous. Serve this this with Ibicenco
Fried Potatoes and Aioli (see pages 293 and 281).

SIRLOIN STEAK (ENTRECÔTE)

Serves 4

❧❧❧❧❧❧❧❧❧❧❧

4 x 250g sirloin steaks
    (about 1kg/2lb 2oz in total)
4 garlic cloves, peeled
Salt and black pepper

Gaucho juice
70g (3oz) sea salt
1 head garlic, cloves peeled
    and crushed
1 tbsp whole black peppercorns,
    crushed in a mortar and pestle
4 whole dried bird's eye chillies
8 thyme sprigs
4 rosemary sprigs
Pared strip of peel from ½ lemon

Rub the steaks with the garlic cloves and sprinkle with salt
and pepper. Discard the garlic and leave the steaks on a plate,
covered in foil, to rest for 1 hour at room temperature.

Meanwhile, make the gaucho juice. Put the salt, garlic,
peppercorns and chillies into a small saucepan with 160ml
(5½fl oz) water. Bring the mixture to the boil and stir until the
salt dissolves completely. Rub the herbs and lemon peel between
your hands to release their fragrance, then stuff them into a
clean glass bottle that has a tight-fitting cork. Carefully pour
the hot liquid into the bottle using a funnel. Seal the bottle with
the cork and swirl to blend the ingredients. (The gaucho juice
can be stored in the fridge for up to 4 weeks.)

Preheat a barbecue grill or griddle pan to hot and place the
steaks on the grill. Splash one side of each steak liberally with
gaucho juice. Grill for 3–4 minutes on each side for medium-
rare, with the splashed side making contact with the grill, then
splash the top of the steaks with more gaucho juice before
turning them. Increase the cooking times to 4–5 minutes on
each side for medium, and 6–7 minutes for well done. To get
nice even char marks, decide in advance how long you want to
cook them on each side and only turn the steaks once. Remove
from the heat and leave to rest for 10 minutes.

How to tell when a steak is done
With a meat thermometer: rare 57°C (135°F), medium-rare
60°C (140°F), medium 68°C (155°F), well done 74°C (165°F).

By touch: Raw meat is squishy. Rare steak is yielding, medium
is springy to the touch, well done gives very little.

Grilled sardines are a Mediterranean classic. When lightly
marinated and stuffed with fresh herbs and lemon peel, they
reach a whole new level of deliciousness.

GRILLED SARDINES STUFFED WITH HERBS AND LEMON

Serves 4

❦ ❦ ❦ ❦ ❦ ❦ ❦ ❦ ❦ ❦ ❦

120ml (4½fl oz) extra virgin
    olive oil
6 garlic cloves, 2 thinly sliced,
    4 thick sliced
12 pared strips of peel
    from 3 lemons
12 rosemary sprigs
12 thyme sprigs
12 whole fresh sardines,
    gutted and rinsed
Salt and black pepper

Put the olive oil and thinly sliced garlic in a jug with a pinch of salt. Leave it to infuse for 15–30 minutes, then remove the garlic.

Gently crush the strips of lemon peel and rosemary and thyme sprigs between your hands to release their aromas, then stuff the cavity of each fish with a sprig of rosemary and thyme and a strip of peel.

Lay the sardines on an oiled baking tray, drizzle with the garlic-infused olive oil and scatter over the 4 thick-sliced garlic cloves. Cover the tray with clingfilm and transfer to the fridge to marinate for 4–6 hours.

Remove the fish from the fridge 30 minutes before cooking, to bring it back to room temperature, and preheat the oven grill to medium. Grill the sardines for 2 minutes, until they curl slightly, then turn them once using silicone-tipped tongs or gloved hands, being careful not to tear the skin of the fish. Grill for a further 2–3 minutes, until the fish is nicely browned and cooked through.

❦ ❦ ❦

Tip: Grilling sardines under an oven grill rather than on a griddle pan or barbecue grill works well, as they don't stick, so the flesh stays intact and keeps moist.

Clams with Serrano ham are a huge favourite at Can Riero. The combination of nutty, earthy ham and fresh sea flavour is uniquely Spanish. Serve with *Pan con Tomate* (see page 285) for an authentic taste of Catalonia.

CLAMS WITH SERRANO

Serves 4 as a starter, 2 as a sharing plate

❧❧❧❧❧❧❧❧❧❧❧

3 tbsp extra virgin olive oil
50g (2oz) sliced Serrano ham,
   cut into matchsticks
1 garlic clove, finely chopped
1kg (2lb 2oz) fresh small clams,
   rinsed and thoroughly
   scrubbed (if wild, soak in
   a bowl of cold water with
   a pinch of salt)
4 tbsp white wine
Small handful flat-leaf parsley
   leaves, finely chopped

Heat the olive oil in a heavy-based frying pan (with a lid) until hot. Add the ham and garlic and fry for 1–2 minutes until the ham is slightly crispy, then add the clams and white wine. Cover the pan tightly with the lid and shake. Cook for 4–5 minutes, shaking occasionally, until nearly all of the clams are open. Remove from the heat, leave the lid on and set the pan aside for a couple of minutes, then remove the lid and transfer the clams to a serving dish, discarding any that remain closed, and sprinkle with parsley. Serve with *Pan con Tomate* (see page 285).

Fideuà is much like paella but takes its name from the small elbow macaroni used in place of rice. The pasta seems to absorb even more flavour. Traditionally, seafood *fideuà* includes white fish but we keep it simple, elegant and very special with just lobster and langoustines. Much like paella, the recipe begins with a chilli base and a *sofregit* – the classic Catalan tomato and onion reduction – a technique taught to me by chefs María and Vicente, whose family-run Restaurante Pinos Playa in Portinatx specialises in fresh seafood caught by their son Juanito.

LOBSTER FIDEUÀ
Serves 6

❦ ❦ ❦ ❦ ❦ ❦ ❦ ❦ ❦ ❦ ❦

You will need: 30cm (12in) ovenproof paella pan or very large, heavy-based ovenproof frying pan

Chilli base
1 dried nora chilli, deseeded and chopped
1 dried ancho chilli, deseeded and chopped

Sofregit
4 tbsp extra virgin olive oil
1 onion, finely chopped
4 garlic cloves, finely chopped
2 Roasted Tomatoes (see page 275), grated
½ green pepper, deseeded and chopped
½ red pepper, deseeded and chopped
Small handful flat-leaf parsley, leaves chopped

2 whole cooked lobsters (about 900g/2lb each), cut into 6 pieces (heads and legs reserved)
1½–2 litres (2½–3½ pints) fish stock
Large pinch saffron threads
18 langoustines, shell on
500g (1lb 2oz) *fideuà* pasta, or skinny elbow macaroni
Aioli, to serve (see page 281)
Lemon wedges, to serve

First, enhance the fish stock. Add the lobster heads and legs to a large saucepan. Add the fish stock and saffron, bring to the boil then reduce the heat and simmer for 20 minutes, uncovered. Strain through a sieve into a heatproof bowl or jug, discard the shells and heads, and set the stock to one side.

To make the chilli base, soak the dried chillies in a heatproof bowl with 250ml (9fl oz) of the boiling fish stock for 30 minutes, then drain, retaining the liquid. Grind the chillies to a paste with a mortar and pestle. Strain the soaking liquid through a fine-mesh sieve into a heatproof measuring jug. Add the chilli paste and whiz with a hand-held blender until smooth. Set aside.

To make the *sofregit*, heat 3 tablespoons of the olive oil in the paella pan or frying pan. Add the onion, garlic, tomatoes, peppers and a handful of parsley and fry over a very low heat for 30 minutes, until soft and golden. Push the mixture to the side of the pan to prevent it burning, then add the remaining olive oil. Add the langoustines and cook for 5–6 minutes until golden, then remove and set aside.

Preheat the oven to 220°C (430°F), gas mark 9.

Add 750ml (25fl oz) of hot fish stock to the pan, mixing it with the *sofregit*, bring to the boil and simmer for 1–2 minutes to infuse the flavours, then add the pasta. Stir in 150ml (5fl oz) of the chilli base and cook for 1–2 minutes. Add the langoustines and continue to cook, stirring gently to distribute the stock. Cook for 6–8 minutes, adding more stock if needed, then add the lobster pieces, nestling them into the pasta. Cook, uncovered, for 2–3 minutes. When the pasta is just *al dente* and the *fideuà* is the desired consistency, remove the pan from the hob. Drizzle the remaining chilli sauce over the top. Bake in the oven for 3–5 minutes, until the edges are slightly caramelised. Serve with aioli and lemon wedges.

Paella, the iconic Spanish holiday dish, is most memorably enjoyed on a beach with a cold jug of sangría. Breaking it down into simple steps, like the *fideuà*, makes it easy to bring Ibiza home. Invite guests over to share this dish and serve it with Mulberry and Peach Cava Sangría (see page 150).

SEAFOOD PAELLA

Serves 6

❦ ❦ ❦ ❦ ❦ ❦ ❦ ❦ ❦ ❦ ❦

You will need: 30cm (12in) paella
  pan or large, heavy-based pan

Chilli base
2 dried nora chillies, deseeded
  and finely chopped
1–1½ litres (1¾–2½ pints) fish stock

Sofregit
80ml (3¼fl oz) extra virgin olive oil
1 onion, finely chopped
½ red pepper and ½ green pepper,
  deseeded and finely chopped
6 garlic cloves, finely chopped
3 large Roasted Tomatoes
  (see page 275), chopped

1½ tsp pimentón dulce
  (sweet paprika)
1 tsp pimentón picante (hot paprika)
Huge pinch saffron threads
6 small squid, or 1 large, cleaned,
  membrane removed, body sliced
  into 3cm (1¼in) rings (tentacles
  left whole)
500g (1lb 2oz) paella rice
300ml (11fl oz) white wine
18 shell-on prawns
18 mussels, scrubbed and debearded
18 fresh clams, scrubbed (soak
  wild in cold water with salt)
1 whole cooked lobster, split
  in half lengthways (optional)
Lemon wedges, to serve
Aioli (see page 281), to serve
Salt and black pepper

To make the chilli sauce, soak the chillies in a heatproof bowl with 80–100ml (3¼–3½fl oz) of the hot fish stock for 30 minutes, then drain, retaining the liquid. Grind the chillies to a paste with a mortar and pestle. Strain the soaking liquid through a fine mesh sieve into a heat-proof measuring jug. Add the chilli paste to the jug, whizz with a hand-held blender till smooth, set aside.

To make the *sofregit*, heat the olive oil in the paella pan or frying pan over a medium-low heat. Add the onion, peppers, garlic and tomatoes and fry for about 20 minutes until soft but not brown. Add the pimentón dulce, pimentón picante and a large pinch of sea salt and cook for 8–10 minutes, uncovered, until the mixture has reduced to a thick sauce.

Bring the remaining stock to the boil in a separate saucepan, reduce the heat and add the saffron. Add the squid to the pan, turn to coat in the sauce, and cook for 2–3 minutes, then remove and set aside

Add the rice to the pan and stir it to coat the grains in the sauce. Fry for 3–4 minutes to lightly toast the rice, then pour in the white wine. Cook for 3–4 minutes, to allow the wine to reduce slightly, then pour enough simmering stock into the pan to just cover the rice. Return the squid to the pan, evenly distributing it and nestling it into the rice, then cook over a low heat for 10–15 minutes, uncovered, gently stirring in more hot stock as needed. Paella, like risotto, requires a bit of judgement when cooking. Taste it to check the texture of the rice and add liquid to reach the desired consistency.

Place the prawns, mussels and clams evenly on top and cook for a further 10 minutes, uncovered, then mix the lobster pieces (if using) into the rice. Remove the pan from the heat and leave to rest for 10 minutes. If you're not using lobster, remove the pan from the heat after the prawns, mussels and clams have had 10 minutes of cooking. Serve with lemon wedges and aioli.

Grilled fish is wonderful with fisherman's potatoes and green herb sauce.
It is easy to cook, indoors or out, but there is something very special about
grilling and eating it at the beach. The old fisherman's method of boiling
potatoes in sea water leaves a delicious trace of salt on the skins once the
liquid evaporates. The trick is to use a heavy-based enamel saucepan
like a Le Creuset, so the potatoes can cook dry without scorching.

GRILLED SEA BREAM (SARGO) WITH GREEN HERB SAUCE AND FISHERMAN'S POTATOES

Serves 4

❦ ❦ ❦ ❦ ❦ ❦ ❦ ❦ ❦ ❦

4 whole wild sea bream
(about 350g/12oz each),
scaled, gutted and cleaned
80ml (3¼fl oz) extra virgin
olive oil
Salt and black pepper

Fisherman's potatoes
700g (1½lb) small new potatoes
3 tbsp coarse sea salt

Green herb sauce
75ml (3fl oz) extra virgin olive oil
3 tbsp sherry vinegar
2 garlic cloves, crushed
2 bird's eye chillies, deseeded
¼ tsp ground cumin
¼ tsp ground coriander
2 tbsp chopped oregano leaves
2 handfuls coriander,
leaves chopped
Handful flat-leaf parsley,
leaves chopped

Scrub the potatoes and put them in a heavy-based (preferably enamel) saucepan with 360ml (12fl oz) cold water, add the salt and bring to the boil. Cook over a medium-high heat for 15–20 minutes, until all the water has evaporated. Pierce a potato to check they are done; if not, add a bit more boiling water and continue cooking. The potatoes should be covered in a light dusting of white salt when the water has evaporated. Remove from the heat and set aside.

For the green herb sauce, put all the ingredients in a measuring jug. Purée with a hand-held blender until smooth, then taste, season with salt and pepper and blend again. Set aside.

Heat a griddle pan over a high heat. Rub the fish all over with olive oil and season with salt and pepper inside and out. Place the fish in the hot pan and cook for 4–5 minutes on the first side. If the fish sticks when you try to turn it, leave it for another minute until it comes away easily. Turn it over and grill it for 4–5 minutes on the other side. Serve immediately, with the green sauce and potatoes.

Granitas are one of the huge pleasures of the hot Mediterranean summer. Cold, fresh and fruity, they are one of the only things I can enjoy eating all day long. It's also a great way to use the abundance of sweet, ripe early summer fruit on Ibiza.

STRAWBERRY GRANITA

Serves 4

❧ ❧ ❧ ❧ ❧ ❧ ❧ ❧ ❧ ❧ ❧

2kg (4lb 4oz) strawberries, hulled
200g (7oz) caster sugar
½ tsp salt
1 tsp good-quality balsamic vinegar

Put 1.5kg (3lb 4oz) of the strawberries in a heavy-based saucepan over a medium-low heat.

Put the remaining 500g (1lb 2oz) of strawberries in a bowl with 50g (2oz) of the sugar, the salt and balsamic vinegar. Set aside to macerate at room temperature.

Add the remaining sugar to the pan of strawberries with 80ml (3¼fl oz) water and stir to combine. Bring to a simmer, then reduce the heat and cook for 10–15 minutes, uncovered, until the strawberries have broken down. Pass the strawberries through a sieve sitting over a heatproof bowl or jug, to separate the juice from the fruit, and press the fruit through the sieve to extract all the juice.

Add the warm strawberry juice to the macerated strawberries and blend the mixture with a hand-held blender until completely smooth. Add a little more salt, balsamic vinegar or sugar to taste. Freeze in an ice-cream maker, according to the manufacturer's instructions, or freeze in a clean baking tray, raking through the mixture with a fork every 30 minutes, until it is fully frozen.

❧ ❧ ❧

Tip: These recipes have been adapted for less-sweet, non-Mediterranean fruit. If on Ibiza, using local fruit, adjust sugar quantities as follows: 75g (3oz) sugar for strawberry, 50g (2oz) for apricot and 25g (1oz) for cherry.

Apricot Granita

❧ ❧ ❧ ❧ ❧ ❧ ❧ ❧ ❧ ❧ ❧ ❧

2kg (4lb 4oz) apricots
½ vanilla pod
150g (5oz) caster sugar
¼ tsp salt
1 tsp brandy or amaretto

❧ ❧ ❧ ❧ ❧ ❧ ❧ ❧ ❧ ❧ ❧

To peel the apricots, cut a cross on the bottom of each and submerge them in boiling water for 30 seconds. The skin will curl slightly and should easily peel off. Remove the stones and quarter the fruit, then put the apricots in a heavy-based saucepan over a medium-low heat. Split the vanilla pod lengthways, scrape out the seeds, and add the seeds and the scraped pod to the apricots. Add the sugar, salt and brandy or amaretto to the pan with 80ml (3¼fl oz) water and bring to a simmer. Reduce the heat and simmer for 8–10 minutes, uncovered, until the apricots have broken down. Pass the apricots through a sieve as on page 134.

Add 500g (1lb 2oz) of the cooked apricots to the sieved juice and blend with a hand-held blender until completely smooth. Freeze as on page 134.

Cherry Granita

❧ ❧ ❧ ❧ ❧ ❧ ❧ ❧ ❧ ❧ ❧ ❧

2kg (4lb 4oz) fresh cherries,
    pitted (about 1.5kg/3lb 4oz once pitted)
¼ tsp salt
100g (3½oz) caster sugar
1 tbsp cassis or kirsch

❧ ❧ ❧ ❧ ❧ ❧ ❧ ❧ ❧ ❧ ❧

Put 1kg (2lb 2oz) of the cherries in a heavy-based saucepan over a medium heat. Add the salt, sugar and 80ml (3¼fl oz) water to the pan and bring to a simmer. Reduce the heat and simmer for 10–12 minutes, uncovered, until the cherries have broken down. Pass the cherries through a sieve as on page 134.

Add the remaining 500g (1lb 2oz) fresh cherries and the cassis or kirsch to the juice and purée until smooth. Freeze as on page 134.

This perfect flavour pairing is an ideal summer treat: cool, simple and sweet. Our Ibiza peaches sun-ripen until they are extremely soft and sweet, so peeling and roasting are just extra steps. This recipe is adapted to peaches from colder climes, where turning on the oven in the summer does not seem hideous and the fruits need a bit more sugar.

PEACHES IN DESSERT WINE

Serves 6

❧ ❧ ❧ ❧ ❧ ❧ ❧ ❧ ❧ ❧ ❧

3 large ripe peaches, peeled,
   pitted and cut into wedges
3–4 tbsp soft light brown sugar
500ml (18fl oz) Moscatel or
   other Spanish dessert wine

Preheat the oven grill to medium. Put the peach wedges in an ovenproof frying pan, cut sides up, and sprinkle liberally with brown sugar. Grill for 3–4 minutes, until the sugar caramelises, then remove.

Meanwhile, bring the wine to the boil in a saucepan. Remove it from the heat as soon as it reaches the boil and pour it over the peaches.

Cover and allow to cool to room temperature before serving, or keep in the fridge for up to 24 hours.

❧ ❧ ❧

Tip: To peel the peaches, cut a cross in the bottom of each peach and submerge them in boiling water for about 30 seconds, until the skin curls away from the fruit. The skin should slip off easily.

Think silk. This sublime cheesecake recipe is adapted from local chef extraordinaire Tim Payne, who serves a version with apricot coulis made from Can Riero's apricots. We love it with fresh mulberries from our friend Vicente's farm, just down the road. Either way, it's great.

MULBERRY CHEESECAKE

Serves 10–12

❧ ❧ ❧ ❧ ❧ ❧ ❧ ❧ ❧ ❧ ❧
❧ ❧ ❧ ❧ ❧ ❧ ❧ ❧ ❧ ❧

You will need: 24cm (9in)
  round springform cake tin

225g (8oz) digestive biscuits
75g (3oz) unsalted butter, melted
800g (1¾lb) cream cheese
100g (3½oz) soured cream
125g (4½oz) caster sugar,
  plus 2–4 tbsp for topping
1 large egg
1 vanilla pod, split lengthways
  and seeds scraped
½ tsp blackberry liqueur
125g (4½oz) mulberries

Preheat the oven to 170°C (340°F), gas mark 4.

To make the base, blitz the biscuits in the bowl of a food processor, or put them in a plastic bag, seal the bag and bash them with a rolling pin. Combine the biscuit crumbs and melted butter in a bowl then press the mixture evenly into the base of the cake tin.

Beat the cream cheese, soured cream, caster sugar, egg and vanilla seeds together in the bowl of a stand mixer or in a bowl with a hand mixer. Pour the mixture onto the cheesecake base and bake for 45–50 minutes. The cake is done when a toothpick inserted into the middle comes out clean and the top is slightly golden. Remove from the oven and leave to cool completely before removing the cheesecake from the tin.

For the topping, combine the sugar in a saucepan with the mulberry liqueur and place over a low heat. Remove the pan from the heat when the sugar has dissolved and leave to cool completely. Gently stir in the mulberries, taking care to not break them up. The fruit can vary widely in sweetness, so taste and add more sugar if desired.

Allow the mulberry mixture to cool completely, then spoon it over the cheesecake. Chill the cake for at least 30–60 minutes before serving.

This recipe idea is from Restaurant Es Torrent, situated on one of the most beautiful private bays on Ibiza's south coast. We go there for the sublime local grilled fish and this, the most divine dessert. I added the mango and the rum, making it almost tropical. It's our non-local guilty pleasure.

CREMA CATALANA WITH PINEAPPLE AND MANGO

Serves 4 (sharing 1 half pineapple each)

❧ ❧ ❧ ❧ ❧ ❧ ❧ ❧ ❧ ❧ ❧

250ml (9fl oz) whole milk
250ml (9fl oz) double cream
1 tsp vanilla bean paste
7 medium egg yolks
80g (3¼oz) caster sugar,
    plus 6 tbsp for topping
10g (⅓oz) cornflour
1 pineapple, very ripe but
    with a firm shell
1 very ripe mango, peeled
1 tsp dark aged rum
Finely grated zest of
    1 lime

Place the milk, cream and vanilla bean paste in a saucepan over a medium heat and heat until the mixture begins to steam.

Meanwhile, put the egg yolks, sugar and cornflour in the bowl of a stand mixer fitted with the whisk attachment and beat for 2–3 minutes until very pale. Alternatively, beat in a mixing bowl with a hand-held electric mixer.

Gradually pour the yolk mixture into the hot cream mixture, stirring continuously with a wooden spoon. Reduce the heat to medium-low and cook, stirring continuously, for 7–10 minutes, until the mixture thickens and coats the back of the spoon. Remove from the heat.

Halve the pineapple lengthways, leaving each half-shell with its leaves intact. Scoop out the fruit, leaving a 0.5cm (¼in)-thick shell. Remove all the 'eyes' then weigh out and roughly chop 50g (2oz) of the pineapple flesh.

Weigh out 50g (2oz) of mango flesh and chop it to the same size as the pineapple pieces. Combine the mango, pineapple, rum and lime zest in a bowl and stir together. Divide the fruit between the pineapple shells and pour half the crema over each. Sprinkle 3 tablespoons of sugar evenly over each half then caramelise the sugar carefully with a blowtorch before serving (each half should be completely covered in caramelised sugar so it takes a good knock to break it).

This is a recipe designed specifically to showcase Ibiza's wonderful early summer fruit. Not too sweet, not too rich, it's traditional Ibiza in its spareness. The elements around the fruit are simple, designed to let the fruit shine. Have it for a light dessert or a fabulous weekend breakfast. Be short with the sugar, it's not meant to be overly sweet. If the flavour of the fruit needs a little help, add a little lemon juice.

ORANGE-SCENTED SUMMER FRUIT SHORTCAKE WITH CHANTILLY CREAM

Serves 6

✦ ✦ ✦ ✦ ✦ ✦ ✦ ✦ ✦ ✦ ✦ ✦

Orange-scented shortcake biscuits
(makes 6 large biscuits)
250g (9oz) plain flour,
   plus extra for dusting
½ tsp fine salt
1 tbsp baking powder
300ml (11fl oz) double cream
Finely grated zest of
   ¼ large orange, plus
   extra for decorating
60g (2½oz) unsalted butter,
   melted

Chantilly cream
120ml (4½fl oz) whipping cream
1 tbsp caster sugar
Splash Grand Marnier

Summer fruit compote
175g (6oz) strawberries,
   hulled and thickly sliced
175g (6oz) mulberries
175g (6oz) cherries, pitted
   and halved
3 tbsp caster sugar, or to taste

For the syrup
50g (2oz) caster sugar
1 tbsp Grand Marnier

Preheat the oven to 190°C (375°F), gas mark 5 and line a baking tray with greaseproof paper.

To make the orange-scented shortcake biscuits, sift together the flour, salt and baking powder into a bowl. Add the cream and orange zest and stir gently until a ball forms. Lightly knead the ball of dough 3–4 times on a floured work surface, with floured hands, then leave it to rest for 5 minutes.

Roll out the dough on a floured surface to a thickness of 2cm (¾in) and cut out rounds with a 4cm (1½in) cutter. Gather the remnants, roll out and re-cut until you have used all the dough.

Place the biscuits on the lined baking tray, brush with melted butter, sprinkle with extra orange zest and bake for 10–12 minutes, until puffed and pale golden. Remove from the oven and leave to cool.

To make the Chantilly cream, whip the cream with a hand mixer in a stainless-steel bowl until it froths, then add the sugar and Grand Marnier and beat for 2–3 minutes until soft peaks form. Transfer to the fridge until ready to serve.

To make the summer fruit compote, gently combine the fruit and sugar in a bowl. Set aside to macerate for 30 minutes.

For the syrup, boil 50ml (2fl oz) water and the sugar in a small saucepan then reduce the heat and simmer until the sugar has dissolved. Remove from the heat, add the Grand Marnier and leave to cool. Taste, adding more liqueur if you like.

To assemble, slice the cooled shortcake biscuits in half horizontally. Poke holes in both sides with a toothpick and drizzle over some of the syrup. Dollop Chantilly cream over the base, add a spoon of the compote and arrange the top half of the biscuit on top. Serve immediately.

Greixonera, the traditional sweet Ibicenco bread pudding, remains hugely popular. It is one of those dishes that inspires fond childhood memories. Though the recipe pretty much sticks to tradition, I do take liberties: adding cherries and almonds. A dish so very good deserves enhancements. Serve it warm or at room temperature, for dessert or for a fabulous brunch.

CHERRY AND ALMOND GREIXONERA

Serves 8

❧ ❧ ❧ ❧ ❧ ❧ ❧ ❧ ❧ ❧ ❧

You will need: 24cm (9in) round or similar square baking dish, about 6cm (3in) deep

Butter, for greasing
500g (1lb 2oz) loaf brioche, torn into bite-sized pieces
130g (4½oz) cherries, pitted and quartered
20g (¾oz) toasted slivered almonds
1 litre (1¾ pints) whole milk (or 500ml/18fl oz milk and 500ml/18fl oz single cream for a richer pudding)
200g (7oz) caster sugar
1 cinnamon stick
Pared strips of peel from 1 lemon
6 large eggs
2 tbsp brandy
¼ tsp salt
55g (2¼oz) soft light brown sugar

Butter a deep baking dish. Put the brioche pieces in the dish and sprinkle the quartered cherries and half the slivered almonds evenly over the bread.

Put the milk, sugar, cinnamon stick and strips of lemon peel in a saucepan and bring to the boil. Remove from the heat and leave to infuse for 15 minutes, then remove the lemon peel and cinnamon stick.

Whisk the eggs, brandy and salt into the milk mixture, then pour this over the bread, cover and transfer to the fridge to chill for 4 hours, or overnight.

Preheat the oven to 170°C (340°F), gas mark 4. Mix the remaining almonds with the brown sugar and sprinkle the mixture over the top of the pudding. Bake for 45–50 minutes, or until the top is golden and a skewer inserted into the middle of the pudding comes out dry.

This recipe has several steps but if you are going to make ice cream, make it sensational – and this one is. Cherry concentrate lends rich flavour and colour to the cream base. The brandied cherries and chocolate are pure elegant decadence. For best results use an electric ice-cream maker with a self-refrigerating compressor feature.

BRANDIED CHERRY ICE CREAM WITH CHOCOLATE CHUNKS

Serves 8

❧ ❧ ❧ ❧ ❧ ❧ ❧ ❧ ❧ ❧

500ml (18fl oz) double cream
250ml (9fl oz) whole milk
6 large egg yolks
150g (5oz) caster sugar
1½ tsp vanilla extract

Cherry concentrate
500g (1lb 2oz) cherries, rinsed and destemmed, but not pitted
1 tsp lemon juice
2 tbsp caster sugar
115g (4oz) dark chocolate (about 60 per cent cocoa solids), roughly chopped
200g (7oz) best-quality brandied cherries, well drained (save the juice from the drained cherries and add a splash to Cava when you entertain)

Pour the cream and milk into a heavy-based saucepan and bring to the boil over a medium heat.

Meanwhile, whisk the egg yolks, sugar and vanilla extract in a large heatproof bowl until pale and thick. Pour the hot cream mixture into the egg yolks, whisking continuously, then strain the mixture through a fine-mesh sieve back into the saucepan and place over a low heat. Cook for 6–8 minutes, stirring continuously and thoroughly with a wooden spoon, ensuring it doesn't stick, until the mixture thickens slightly – it should coat the back of the spoon. Remove from the heat and immediately pour the custard into a clean heatproof bowl. Cover the custard with clingfilm, ensuring the film touches the surface of the custard so that no skin forms, allow to cool to room temperature and then chill for 3–4 hours.

Meanwhile, to make the cherry concentrate, put the cherries, lemon juice, sugar and 120ml (4½fl oz) of water in a saucepan. Bring to the boil then reduce the heat and simmer slowly for 10–12 minutes, until the cherries are soft and the liquid has reduced to a light syrup. Press through a fine-mesh sieve over a heatproof bowl, to extract all the juice, and set aside to cool.

Combine the cooled cherry juice concentrate with the chilled custard and churn in an ice-cream maker according to the manufacturer's instructions. When the custard reaches the soft ice cream stage, stir in the chocolate chunks and brandied cherries. Transfer to the freezer for 2 hours until set hard.

❧ ❧ ❧

Tip: Some ice-cream makers have 'mix-in' features that allow additions in the last 5 minutes of processing. Because the quantity of chocolate and cherries exceeds the settings of most standard ice-cream makers, it is best to stir them in after processing.

Sangría, the iconic Spanish libation, lovely, light, cold and fruity, is wonderful on long hot Ibiza summer afternoons. Traditionally sangría is made with red wine, a splash of brandy, lemonade or fruit juice, sugar and sliced oranges, lemons, apples and sometimes grapes. Modern sangría can be made with a white wine or Cava base, and it's trendy to use a variety of fabulous fruits: berries, kiwi, pineapple – anything goes. If using sugar, add a little at a time, to taste. This recipe uses Cava with mulberries and peaches; a fabulous seasonal pairing of both colour and flavour. I finish it with blackberry liqueur and brandy.

MULBERRY AND PEACH CAVA SANGRÍA

Serves 6

❧ ❧ ❧ ❧ ❧ ❧ ❧ ❧ ❧ ❧ ❧

750ml (25fl oz) bottle
  Cava, chilled
150ml (5fl oz) good-quality peach
  juice (no added sugar), or fresh
100ml (3½fl oz) good-quality
  white grape juice (no added
  sugar), or fresh
100ml (3½fl oz) blackberry
  liqueur
50ml (2fl oz) brandy
2 ripe peaches, peeled and sliced
75g (3oz) mulberries or fresh
  blackberries
1 orange, peeled and sliced
  into segments (optional)
Small ice cubes or crushed ice

Mix the peach and grape juices, blackberry liqueur and brandy together in a large pitcher. Add all the fruit, mix and fill a third of the way up with ice cubes. Open the Cava and pour into the pitcher. Mix, then top with ice to serve. Pour so that each glass gets a scoop of each fruit and ice.

❧ ❧ ❧

Tip: Ibiza mulberries are incredibly sweet, making sugar optional. If using British mulberries, sugar will likely be necessary. Picking mulberries is great fun but turns hands purple. To get the stains off, pick a handful of green berries, crush, and use like soap to scrub your hands. Amazingly, the stain goes.

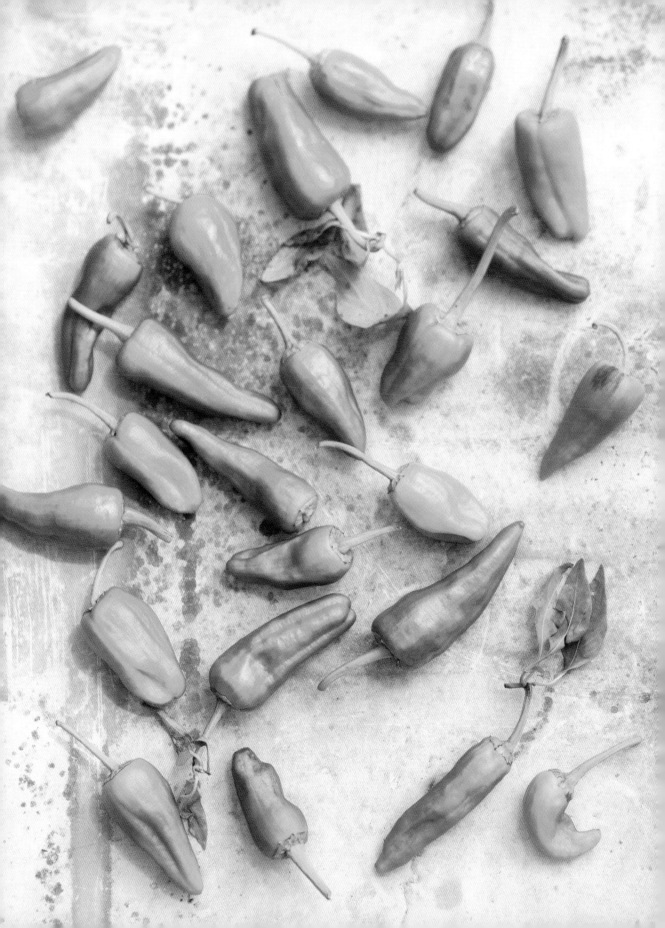

AUTUMN

Autumn, like spring, is long and luxurious, a time of renewal on Ibiza. The island, parched from summer sun, grows vibrant and green from intense rains that leave scrubbed blue skies. Gardens are again prolific: lettuces, herbs, green beans, all things too delicate to survive the heat, grow back. Summer's tomatoes, peppers and aubergines can keep cropping into October and even November. Spinach, pumpkins, pomegranates, apples, beans and sweet potatoes are all in harvest, too. Hunting wild mushrooms, our very favourite of all foraging, begins just after the first cold rain.

This is the season of Ibiza's ancient, mythic fruits: olives and figs. There are olive trees thought to be over 1000 years old on the island. My friend Vicente has one more than 5 metres in diameter on his land, pocked with scars deep enough for his chickens to roost in (see photo pages 172–173). Across the island, farmers harvest the olives to press into smooth, fruity extra virgin olive oil. Fig trees, with their gnarled branches and jewel-toned fruit, are equally emblematic of the season. Both purple and green figs grow in abundance at Can Riero; for us, they are the fruit that most represents the flavour and texture of autumnal Ibiza. We use them in dishes both sweet and savoury, hot and cold, and eat them right off the tree.

With this endless bounty, Can Riero's kitchen is at its inspired best, roasting tomatoes and peppers, pickling, drying figs and preserving quince into membrillo. Ibiza's *campo* is alive with activity, too: gathering, drying, curing, storing, preparing and planting. Autumn is a time of revival, harvest and preservation. A time to reconnect to the kitchen and the land.

AUTUMN CHARCUTERIE PLATE WITH SPICED NUTS

Serves 4

❦ ❦ ❦ ❦ ❦ ❦ ❦ ❦ ❦ ❦

200g (7oz) Mahón curado
   or Pecorino cheese
200 (7oz) rosemary-rind
   Can Caus goat's cheese, or
   other aged goat's cheese
150g (5oz) crackers
200g (7oz) *cecina* or bresaola
150g (5oz) *chistorra de Nevarra*,
   or other paprika-spiced
   pork sausage
150g (5oz) *Llonganissa Pagesa*,
   or other cured pork sausage
   spiced with black pepper
8 fresh, ripe green or black figs
200g (7oz) Fig Chutney
   (see page 280)
100g (3½oz) Spiced Nuts
   (see below)
100g Membrillo, shop bought
   or homemade (see page 277)

❦ ❦ ❦ ❦ ❦ ❦ ❦ ❦ ❦ ❦

Spiced nuts
   (makes 1kg/2lb 2oz)
2 egg whites
5–6 sprigs rosemary,
   leaves finely chopped
Small handful thyme,
   leaves finely chopped
4 sage leaves, finely chopped
2 fresh red chillies, deseeded
   and finely chopped
1 tbsp pimentón dulce
   (sweet paprika)
2 tsp salt flakes
1kg (2lb 2oz) mixed nuts
   and seeds, such as walnuts,
   almonds, pumpkin seeds
   and sunflower seeds

Autumn is a lovely time for Spanish charcuterie, of which many great varieties are available internationally. The selection criteria for this platter is similar to that for spring; the number of meats should be three or five, of different shape, size and texture and flavour. Here we use a new favourite find: *cecina*, a dried, cured and smoked leg of beef from León, north-west Spain. Dark red and streaked with tiny veins of fat, it is slightly salty, deeply smoky and has a meaty, earthy flavour. Serve, like a good Serrano ham, sliced extremely thin with bread or fruit. The figs not only play well with *cecina* but also set the seasonal tone. Here, too, is *Llonganissa Pagesa*, a dried pork sausage from the Catalan Pyrenees, made with red wine and black pepper, so it is rich and peppery with a unique back note: sweet, musty and fruity. Slice it like a salami. For a different shape we added a thinner dried sausage, *chistorra de Navarra*, from the Navarran Pyrenees. This classic pork sausage, sometimes a mix of beef and pork, is flavoured with garlic and paprika.

For cheese, we selected two that work well with autumn condiments. Mahón curado, a strong cow's milk cheese, and an Ibiza Can Caus goat's cheese: milder but with a dried rosemary rind. The aromatic sweet membrillo is divine with the sharp nutty tang of the Mahón curado, and the sweet acid of the fig chutney works well with either cheese. The herb-roasted nuts add a bit of crunch. Make these in a large quantity as they are a great quick bite straight from the bowl.

SPICED NUTS

Preheat the oven to 170°C (340°F), gas mark 4.

Whisk the egg whites in a clean, grease-free bowl to medium-soft peaks, either by hand or using a stand mixer.

Combine the herbs, chilli, spices and salt and fold into the egg whites. Stir in the nuts until they are evenly coated with the egg.

Spread the nuts on a non-stick baking tray and bake for 20 minutes. Remove from the oven and use a spatula to scrape up the nuts, breaking up any chunks, then toss and return to the oven for a further 20–25 minutes, until they are completely crisp. Remove from the oven and leave to cool. The nuts will keep for up to 4 days in an airtight container in a cool, dry place.

SPANISH HAM – PATA NEGRA AND SERRANO

Rich dark red and elegantly marbled, Spanish ham -- *jamón ibérico* – is one of the world's great culinary delicacies. It gives way in the mouth like exquisite chocolate and is considered by many to be the finest ham, bar none. *Jamón ibérico*, also known as *pata negra* ('black foot') is made from black-hooved Iberian pigs. This ancient breed is as integral to Spanish food culture as olives or oranges. *Jamón ibérico* has PDO (Protected Designation of Origin) status, which means that, like Parmesan or Champagne, it can only be produced in specific regions under strict conditions.

There are three classifications based on the breed purity, diet and the conditions under which the pigs are raised. The finest is *jamón ibérico de bellota*, produced from pigs that are at least 75 per cent Iberian (just 5 per cent of *bellota* comes from 100 per cent pure Iberian pigs). They roam free on the oak-studded grasslands (*dehesas*) of southern Spain and eat only wild food, mostly acorns (*bellota*) which lend their name and unique flavour. A leg of bellota takes a minimum of 600 days to produce; this is reflected in the price, which can exceed €100 per kilo. Cut razor thin, it literally melts in the mouth; its flavour is nutty, salty and meaty. Nearly as divine, but less dear, is *jamón ibérico de recebo*. Like *bellota*, it comes from free-range pigs that are at least 75 per cent pure Iberian, but their diet is supplemented with grains. The third classification, *jamón ibérico de cebo de campo*, is grain-fed, meaning the pigs can be slaughtered younger, thus shortening the production process. Aficionados can tell the difference between the three grades, but all versions of *jamón ibérico* are a delicacy.

Jamón serrano ('of the mountains') is dry-cured ham produced from white pigs. One of Europe's finest hams, Serrano is defined by its method of production. According to regulations governing its TSG status (Traditional Specialities Guaranteed) it must be salted, washed, set, dried and cured for a minimum of 210 days. The Fundación Serrano (Serrano Foundation) has two classifications: Reserva, aged between 12 and 15 months; and Gran Reserva, cured for at least 15 months.

A much-loved tapa found throughout Barcelona and the heart of Catalonia, these aubergine chips are divinely sinful. We use organic aubergines and our own honey to make this version of *berenjenas con miel y canela.*

FRIED AUBERGINE CHIPS WITH CINNAMON HONEY

Serves 4

❦ ❦ ❦ ❦ ❦ ❦ ❦ ❦ ❦ ❦ ❦

2–3 small, firm aubergines, cut
　into thin slices lengthways
　(about 3mm thick)
1 tsp salt
75g (3oz) plain flour
2 pinches cayenne pepper
300ml (11fl oz) light olive oil
Freshly ground black pepper

Cinnamon honey
150g (5oz) runny honey
⅛–¼ tsp ground cinnamon

Place the aubergine slices in a bowl, season with the salt, toss and set aside for 20 minutes, then rinse briefly and pat dry with kitchen paper. Lay the ribbons on pieces of kitchen paper, separated out so they are not touching, and leave to air dry for 30 minutes.

Meanwhile, combine the honey and cinnamon in a bowl and set aside.

Place the flour in a shallow bowl and season it with salt, pepper and the cayenne pepper. Heat the olive oil in a deep, heavy-based frying pan until it reaches 180°C (350°F) on a thermometer.

Dredge the aubergine slices in the seasoned flour and fry them a few at a time (they will stick together if you overcrowd the pan) for 2–3 minutes, until lightly golden. Remove with a spider or slotted spoon and transfer to a plate lined with kitchen paper to drain.

When all the aubergines are fried, check the oil is still at 180°C (350°F), then fry the aubergines for another 1–2 minutes, in batches, until crisp. Remove and drain on kitchen paper again, then drizzle with cinnamon honey and salt to serve.

On cool autumn days there is no better snack (*almuerzo*) than *coca*, a traditional Catalonian flatbread. The versatile staple is made with either olive oil or lard and is topped with meat, fish or vegetables; or with sugar as a base for sweet toppings. I first tasted *coca ibicenca* while baking bread with my friends Catalina and Vicente in Sant Carles. Catalina pinched off some dough, massaged it in a bit more olive oil and made the coca while we waited for the bread, finishing it with Hierbas Ibicencas, Ibiza's unique digestive liqueur. It seems every grandfather has a secret recipe. Bottles are stuffed with seven types of dried wild herbs then filled with a blend of anisette and left to steep.

COCA IBICENCA

Makes 8 coca

❧ ❧ ❧ ❧ ❧ ❧ ❧ ❧ ❧ ❧ ❧

650ml (22fl oz) tepid water
60ml (2½fl oz) extra virgin
   olive oil, plus extra
   for brushing
1 tbsp caster sugar
2 x 7g packets (4½ tsp)
   dried yeast
800g (1¾lb) strong white flour,
   plus extra for dusting
200g (7oz) fine semolina flour,
   plus extra for dusting
1 tsp salt

Topping
60g (2½oz) pine nuts
100g (3½oz) soft light
   brown sugar
60ml (2½fl oz) Hierbas
   Ibicencas liqueur
salt and black pepper

❧ ❧ ❧

Tip: If you can't get hold of Hierbas Ibicencas liqueur, drizzle the breads with anisette and sprinkle with finely chopped thyme.

Combine the tepid water with the oil and sugar in a bowl. Sprinkle over the yeast and set aside for 5–10 minutes to allow the yeast to activate. The mixture should froth.

Combine the flours and salt in a separate bowl. Pour the yeast mixture into the flour mixture in a slow, steady stream, mixing as you go. Incorporate the liquid well, scraping any flour from the edges of the bowl and mixing it in.

Bring the mixture together to form a rough dough then turn it out onto a floured board or work surface and knead for 3–4 minutes, until the dough is smooth. Sprinkle it with extra flour if it is too sticky to handle easily. Shape the dough into a ball and put it into a large oiled bowl (big enough to allow it to double in size). Cover the bowl with clingfilm and put it in the fridge for 4–6 hours, until the dough is about double the size. If you are short on time, leave the dough to rise at room temperature, covered, for an hour or so.

Preheat the oven to 180°C (350°F) gas mark 4 and dust a baking tray with semolina.

Once the dough has risen, remove the clingfilm and knock it back, then knead it for a couple of minutes. Brush the dough with oil and sprinkle with salt and pepper. Sprinkle the pine nuts and brown sugar over the prepared dough. Set it on the baking tray and bake for 8–10 minutes until the bread is puffed and golden. Remove from the oven, drizzle with the Hierbas and serve.

Traditional Roasted Red Pepper and Onion Coca

This is the real Ibiza classic and one of my very favourites. It is important to thinly slice the vegetables here and roast them at a high heat, as the edges need to be slightly charred.

❧ ❧ ❧ ❧ ❧ ❧ ❧ ❧ ❧ ❧ ❧

3 red peppers. halved, deseeded
   and sliced into matchsticks
2 onions, halved and sliced into
   thin half moons
2–3 tbsp extra virgin olive oil
1–2 tbsp salt
1 x quantity *Coca Ibicenca* dough
   (see page 162)

❧ ❧ ❧ ❧ ❧ ❧ ❧ ❧ ❧ ❧ ❧

Preheat the oven to 200°C (400°F), gas mark 6.

Put the peppers and onions on a baking tray and toss with olive oil and salt. Roast for 10–12 minutes, until soft and juicy, lightly golden and slightly charred at the edges.

Sprinkle the roasted vegetables over the rolled-out, prepared dough and bake in the oven for 10 minutes. The crust should be crisp and the peppers and onions slightly charred but not mushy.

Apple, Queso Azul and Walnut Coca

We grow several varieties of apples at Can Riero that ripen from July right through to September. This is a great way to use them on an early autumn day.

❧ ❧ ❧ ❧ ❧ ❧ ❧ ❧ ❧ ❧ ❧

½ apple, peeled, cored and
   very thinly sliced
Small handful queso azul
   (Spanish blue cheese), crumbled
1 x quantity *Coca Ibicenca* dough
   (see page 162)
Handful toasted walnuts, chopped

❧ ❧ ❧ ❧ ❧ ❧ ❧ ❧ ❧ ❧ ❧

Preheat the oven. Arrange the apple slices and cheese on the rolled-out, prepared dough then bake in the oven for 8 minutes.

Remove from the oven, sprinkle with chopped walnuts and return to the oven and bake for another 2–3 minutes, until the crust is golden, the apples are slightly crisped and the cheese has melted.

Rovellon or Chestnut Mushroom Coca

If rovellons are not available, use a meaty mushroom, like a chestnut or a portobello. They have a nice bite and not much water, so will not go spongy.

❧ ❧ ❧ ❧ ❧ ❧ ❧ ❧ ❧ ❧ ❧

3 tbsp olive oil
4 garlic cloves, peeled and smashed
2 sprigs rosemary
200g rovellon or chestnut mushrooms,
   thinly sliced
1 x quantity *Coca Ibicenca* dough
   (see page 162)
Chopped flat-leaf parsley,
   to serve (optional)
Salt and black pepper

❧ ❧ ❧ ❧ ❧ ❧ ❧ ❧ ❧ ❧ ❧

Preheat the oven.
   Heat the olive oil in a heavy-based frying pan, add the garlic and rosemary, turn the heat down and sauté lightly for about 10 minutes, not browning the garlic but flavouring the oil.
   Remove the aromatics, reheat the oil and add the mushrooms, sprinkle with salt and pepper. Sauté until soft, but *al dente*, about 5 minutes.
   Sprinkle the mushrooms over the rolled-out, prepared dough and bake in the oven for 10 minutes. The crust should be crisp and the mushrooms slightly charred but not mushy. Sprinkle with chopped parsley to serve, if you like.

Roasted Tomato Coca

Roasted tomato and fresh thyme is a classic flavour duo. To me, moving from light, leafy summer herbs to the richer, earthier thyme is a real sign that autumn has arrived.

❧ ❧ ❧ ❧ ❧ ❧ ❧ ❧ ❧ ❧ ❧

175g Roasted Tomato halves (see page 275)
2 large pinches chopped fresh thyme
1 x quantity *Coca Ibicenca* dough (see page 162)
75g cured Mahón or Parmesan cheese,
   very finely grated
Salt and black pepper

❧ ❧ ❧ ❧ ❧ ❧ ❧ ❧ ❧ ❧ ❧

Preheat the oven.
   Combine the tomato halves with the salt, pepper and fresh thyme and mix gently so as not to break up the tomatoes.
   Arrange the tomatoes over the rolled-out, prepared dough. Sprinkle with cheese and bake in the oven for 10 minutes until the crust is crisp.

Picada means chopped and in Catalan cooking it describes a base of nuts, herbs and dried bread used to thicken soups and stews. My interpretation of this classic lets the delicious flavours of the nuts and herbs shine, pairing them with cheeses to make versatile, pesto-like sauces. The secret is to balance the flavours. Strong herbs such as rosemary and sage can overpower; use them lightly and pair with creamy nuts such as cashews. Gentle herbs complement robust cheeses. Ultimately, *picadas* are about personal preference. Try a couple then tweak to your taste.

PINE NUT, PARSLEY, SAGE, ROSEMARY AND THYME PICADA

Makes 120–180g (4½–6oz)

❦❦❦❦❦❦❦❦❦❦❦

60–120ml (2½–4½fl oz)
  extra virgin olive oil
Large bunch flat-leaf parsley,
  leaves chopped
2 sprigs rosemary, leaves chopped
Handful thyme, leaves chopped
8 sage leaves, de-stemmed
  and veins removed
40g (1½oz) pine nuts, toasted
1 dried red chilli, deseeded
  and chopped
Salt and black pepper

Put all the ingredients into the bowl of a food processor, starting with just 60ml (2½fl oz) of the olive oil. Pulse until amalgamated, adding more oil if necessary, until the *picada* resembles a thick, slightly coarse pesto. Alternatively, put all the ingredients in a high-sided container and use a hand-held blender to combine.

Pine Nut, Rocket and Parmesan with Garlic Picada

❦❦❦❦❦❦❦❦❦❦❦

60–120ml (2½–4½fl oz) extra virgin olive oil
80g (3¼oz) rocket
40g (1½oz) pine nuts, toasted
3 small garlic cloves, chopped
75g (3oz) Parmesan cheese, chopped
Salt and black pepper

❦❦❦❦❦❦❦❦❦❦❦

Prepare the *picada* by combining all the ingredients as above.

Almond, Coriander, Lemon Zest and Garlic Picada

❦❦❦❦❦❦❦❦❦❦❦

60–120ml (2½–4½fl oz) extra virgin olive oil
2 garlic cloves, chopped
Large bunch coriander, leaves picked
40g (1½oz) blanched almonds, toasted and chopped
Grated zest of 1 lemon
Salt and black pepper

❦❦❦❦❦❦❦❦❦❦❦

Prepare the *picada* by combining all the ingredients as above.

OLIVE OIL

Olive oil is the most emblematic food of the Mediterranean, and on Ibiza it is second only to salt in its importance as a staple of local cuisine. Gnarled, centuries-old olive trees rise from the red earth of the *campo* like ancient sculptures. Their silvery leaves shimmer as a counterpoint to the deeper greens of pine and grass. Come autumn, neat rows of cultivated olive groves come to life as harvesters shake down the ripe green and glossy black fruit.

Ibicenco families have made olive oil for thousands of years, hand-pressing and storing the oil for their own use. Local producers who adhere to strict guidelines on irrigation, fertilisation, pesticide use, harvest and production techniques can earn 'Oli d'E' certification. This label guarantees that the olive oil is extra virgin, produced completely through organic or sustainable methods, and is made only from olives grown on Ibiza.

Some of Ibiza's producers take sustainability even further. At Oleoteca Ses Escoles, where Can Miquel Guasch oil is produced, and Joan Benet, both dehydrate olive pulp and use it to fertilise the groves. They also grind the discarded pits and press them into fuel for free-standing burners.

Ibiza's oil output is tiny compared to that of the rest of the Mediterranean but its quality is gaining international attention. Oliada, the regulatory association's own-label oil made using fruit from all the island's producers, was awarded a star at the 2013 Great Taste Awards in London for its intense fruity, spicy, bitter flavour.

Olive oil is ideal for every kind of cooking: I use it as a base for marinades and sauces, to drizzle over cheese or charcuterie plates, to dress salads, grill meat and vegetables, and to preserve artichoke hearts or roasted peppers. Along with salt, vinegar and lemon juice, it is an irreplaceable ingredient in the Can Riero larder.

Ibiza's fabulous prawns are deep orange-red with a distinctive, delicate, salty-sweet flavour. They are available fresh at the fishmongers in the summer and autumn months and are easy to spot as they're the most expensive (but well worth it). To maximise their unique flavour we simply poach them in olive oil – a popular technique in Ibiza. Cook them gently and until opaque; their flavour and texture are best when barely done.

GAMBAS (PRAWNS) WITH CHILLI AND GARLIC

Serves 4 as a starter, 2 as a sharing dish

❧ ❧ ❧ ❧ ❧ ❧ ❧ ❧ ❧ ❧ ❧

120ml (4½fl oz) extra virgin
  olive oil
6 garlic cloves, cut into
  paper-thin slices
2 dried red chillies, deseeded
  and cut into quarters, or
  a pinch of red chilli flakes
500g (1lb 2oz) shelled prawns
  (heads off), or 1kg (2lb 2oz)
  whole prawns, peeled, heads
  and digestive tracts removed
Salt and black pepper
1 baguette, or other crusty
  bread, toasted, to serve

Place the olive oil, garlic and chillies in a small saucepan and heat slowly until the oil reaches simmering point. Remove the pan from the heat and leave to infuse for 30 minutes, reheat the oil then add the prawns and cook over a low heat for 5–10 minutes, until the prawns are just opaque.

Put the prawns and oil in a heavy, heated ovenproof dish (to hold the heat) and serve with slices of toasted bread.

Using thawed, frozen, cooked octopus increases the tenderness of its meat. Here the marinade clings to the surface of the dense-fleshed octopus, giving it a divine flavourful char. Grilled lemon is a perfect accompaniment here; its slightly caramelised sweetness is less harsh than raw lemon.

GRILLED OCTOPUS WITH LEMON, GARLIC AND OLIVE OIL

Serves 6

❧ ❧ ❧ ❧ ❧ ❧ ❧ ❧ ❧ ❧ ❧

6 garlic cloves, crushed
2 fresh red chillies, deseeded and chopped
3 lemons, halved
Pared strips of peel from ½ lemon
Juice of ½ lemon
120ml (4½fl oz) extra virgin olive oil
1kg (2lb 2oz) cooked octopus tentacles
Salt and black pepper
1 loaf crusty white bread, to serve

Divide the garlic, chillies, lemon halves, peel and juice and oil between two large resealable freezer bags and mix well. Add the octopus tentacles and toss them in the bags, massaging the octopus in the marinade to coat it thoroughly. Transfer the bags to the fridge and leave to marinate for at least 12 hours.

Preheat the barbecue grill or a griddle pan, and while it's heating up, grill the lemon halves from the marinade, cut side down, for 4–5 minutes until they have visible grill marks.

When the grill is hot, cook the marinated octopus for 5–8 minutes, basting it with marinade, until it is lightly charred and warmed through. Transfer to a serving platter and season with salt and pepper.

Serve with the grilled lemon halves and crusty bread.

❧ ❧ ❧

Tip: A cast-iron grill pan works nearly as well; just make sure to heat the pan thoroughly and oil the lemon and octopus well.

Burrata is not just for summer's fresh tomatoes and basil. This recipe makes wonderful use of it: roasted aubergine, fennel and pepper make the perfect pedestal for burrata. The creamy cheese melts lightly over the hot vegetables, enriching the roasted red pepper sauce and bringing the whole dish together beautifully.

ROASTED AUBERGINE, RED PEPPER AND FENNEL WITH BURRATA

Serves 4

❦ ❦ ❦ ❦ ❦ ❦ ❦ ❦ ❦ ❦ ❦

3 medium aubergines, cut
    into 2.5cm (1in) thick slices
2 fennel bulbs, outer
    layers removed
1 tbsp extra virgin olive oil,
    plus extra for greasing
500g (1lb 2oz) Roasted Red
    Pepper Sauce (see page 283)
2 roasted red peppers, quartered
    and deseeded (shop-bought
    or homemade – see page 274)
40g (1½oz) Mahón curado
    or Pecorino cheese, grated
500g (1lb 2oz) burrata
    (2 x 250g/9oz balls)
Salt and black pepper

Preheat the oven to 180°C (350°F), gas mark 4.

Place the aubergine slices in a bowl, season with salt on both sides and set aside for 20 minutes, then drain and pat dry with kitchen paper.

Slice the fennel bulbs thinly lengthways from the bulb end.

Toss the aubergines and fennel in the olive oil, arrange on a baking tray and roast for 25-30 minutes until tender and golden at the edges.

Meanwhile, grease a casserole dish with oil and pour in enough of the roasted red pepper sauce to just cover the bottom. Layer the roasted aubergine, fennel and roasted peppers in the dish, putting sauce, salt, pepper and a sprinkling of grated cheese between each layer. Top with the remaining grated cheese. Bake for 20–25 minutes, until the vegetables are tender and the cheese is melted and golden, then remove.

Slice a cross in the top of each burrata. Pinch the cheese from the bottom to squeeze out the soft centre and nestle it into the warm vegetables before serving.

Fresh cheese or ricotta is hugely popular all over Spain, and on Ibiza, too. We use a gorgeous sheep's milk one from Can Caus, though any ricotta will do. It's all in the black pepper and lemon – use plenty of both – and, of course, salt. The layer mix should be seasoned enough to stand on its own, like all the components of the dish. This recipe calls for roasting the aubergine rather than shallow frying it, so that it gets a bit crispy around the edges, yet stays soft on the inside without absorbing too much oil. The end result has less fat and, to me, better flavour.

AUBERGINE GRATINADA WITH LEMON PEPPER RICOTTA

Serves 4

❧ ❧ ❧ ❧ ❧ ❧ ❧ ❧ ❧ ❧ ❧

2 medium aubergines, cut lengthways into 1cm (½in) thick slices

250g (9oz) ricotta

Grated zest of 1 lemon

1 tsp salt

¾ tsp freshly ground black pepper

350g (12oz) Roasted Tomato Sauce (see page 282)

125g (4½oz) mozzarella, sliced into rounds

40g (1½oz) Mahón curado or Parmesan cheese, grated

Extra virgin olive oil, for greasing

Salt and black pepper

Preheat the oven to 220°C (430°F), gas mark 7.

Place the aubergine slices in a bowl, season with salt on both sides and set aside for 20 minutes, then drain and pat dry with kitchen paper.

Meanwhile, mix the ricotta in a bowl with the lemon zest, salt and pepper.

Brush a baking sheet with olive oil and sprinkle it with salt and pepper. Put the aubergines on the sheet, brush them with olive oil and roast them for 15–20 minutes, until the insides are soft and the edges crisp.

Lightly grease a 23cm (9in) glass or ceramic baking dish with oil and cover the bottom with 100g (3½oz) of the roasted tomato sauce. Arrange half of the aubergine slices in a snug layer in the bottom of the tin. Spread the peppery lemon ricotta over them in an even layer, then top with the remaining aubergine slices and pour over the remaining sauce. Top with the mozzarella slices and grated cheese, then bake for 20–30 minutes, until the cheese is melted and golden. Remove from the oven and serve warm.

❧ ❧ ❧

Tip: This is a great 'while you're at it, make two' dish: one to eat, one to freeze. Our aubergines tend to explode in the early autumn, so we make several of these at a time. It is nice to have these on hand for those days when cooking is just not possible. If freezing, stop after assembling and wrap the dish up well.

MUSHROOM FORAGING

Foraging is one of the great pleasures of life on Ibiza, and rovellons (saffron milk caps or red pine mushrooms), the most prominent local edible mushroom, are a true culinary prize. The seasonal change in the forest is staggering as the rain brings out the cool, clean, rich scent of pure earth. After the first cool autumn rains, Ibicencos take to the woods for the hunt. Each hunter has a favourite spot. If you are lucky enough to be invited along on the hunt, do not reveal the location to anyone, or return on your own.

There is an etiquette to foraging rovellons: gently brush aside the leaves, needles and earth that obscure them, but don't disturb the forest floor. When you find one, check for the trademark dark red gill on the underside – when scraped, it is blood red. Cut the mushroom cleanly with a sharp knife, leaving some stem intact, then replace the ground cover to promote next season's growth. Above all, watch your step: a crushed rovellon is a missed opportunity.

There are two steps to perfectly cooked mushrooms:

⚘ Clean the mushrooms with a soft-bristled brush, damp paper towel or cloth. Don't wash them, as water makes mushrooms spongy.

⚘ Cook the mushrooms according to size and texture, beginning with the largest and most dense. The smaller, delicate mushrooms require little cooking, so add them at the end when the sauce has cooked down.

Wild mushrooms with brandy are absolutely sublime, and a personal favourite. Earthy, rich and moist, they are the embodiment of the cool rains with which they arrive. Served on toast, they make a great shared dish. They are also perfect as a side dish to rare beef fillet, roast chicken or slow-roasted leg of lamb. We eat them as often as we can when they are in season and at their very best.

WILD MUSHROOMS WITH BRANDY CREAM ON TOAST

Serves 4

❧ ❧ ❧ ❧ ❧ ❧ ❧ ❧ ❧ ❧ ❧ ❧

3 tbsp extra virgin olive oil, plus extra for drizzling
3 tbsp butter
2 garlic cloves, finely chopped
500g (1lb 2oz) mixed wild mushrooms, cut into even bite-sized pieces
4 tbsp brandy
1 tbsp chopped thyme leaves
Pinch cayenne pepper
60ml (2½fl oz) single cream
Salt and black pepper
4 thick slices dense-textured bread, such as Ibicenco *pan payés* or sourdough, to serve

Heat the olive oil and butter in a frying pan until it sizzles when you add a drop of water. Add the garlic and the thickest, densest mushrooms and fry for 1–2 minutes, stirring, then add all the remaining mushrooms (except the most delicate ones). Add half the brandy, the thyme leaves, cayenne and a pinch each of salt and pepper. Shake the pan to distribute the ingredients evenly around the pan and cook for 2–3 minutes until the brandy has evaporated, then transfer the mushrooms to a bowl.

Place the frying pan back over the heat and add the remaining brandy. Light it, to burn off the alcohol, then add the cream and bring to the boil. Simmer for 4–5 minutes until it starts to thicken, then season with salt and black pepper. Return the cooked mushrooms to the pan and add the delicate mushrooms. Shake the pan to coat the mushrooms thoroughly with the brandy cream and cook for 2–3 minutes until hot through.

Meanwhile, toast the bread. Arrange the toast on plates and drizzle with olive oil and salt. Top the toast with the mushrooms and serve immediately.

❧ ❧ ❧

Tip: Add quarter of a teaspoon of grated lemon zest, or more to taste, to freshen up the mushroom sauce if it tastes too rich and heavy.

The Latin name for rovellon, *Lactarius deliciosus,* is well deserved. These mushrooms have a glorious flavour: light and earthy, just like the forest smells, a true delicacy. Meaty and low in moisture, they do not need a lot of cooking time to condense their flavour. Garlic is a great way to enhance a mushroom but it is used here with a light touch, to let the rovellons' distinctive flavour shine.

ROVELLONS A LA PLANCHA

Serves 4 as a tapa

❧ ❧ ❧ ❧ ❧ ❧ ❧ ❧ ❧ ❧ ❧

1 garlic clove, thinly sliced
3–4 tbsp extra virgin olive oil
300g (11oz) rovellon or baby
    portobello mushrooms
Salt flakes and black pepper

Put the sliced garlic and olive oil in a bowl and set aside to infuse for 30 minutes, then remove the garlic.

Slice the mushroom stems off at the base and brush the caps gently to remove any dirt.

Heat 3 tablespoons of the oil in a cast-iron griddle pan over a medium-high heat, then add the mushrooms, gill side up. Cook for 2–3 minutes, pressing the mushrooms gently with a spatula so they brown evenly. Turn them over and add another tablespoon of oil, if necessary. Cook for a further 1–2 minutes. The gills should remain intact, not mashed.

Season with salt and pepper and serve as a tapa.

This simple oven dish uses a braise to create a juicy and tender chicken, finishing with a high-heat roast to crisp up the skin. It's a great technique for a near-perfect, normally hard-to-achieve result: juicy, tender and crisp.

CHICKEN WITH DRIED FIGS

Serves 6

❦ ❦ ❦ ❦ ❦ ❦ ❦ ❦ ❦ ❦ ❦

4 tbsp extra virgin olive oil
1 large organic, free-range
　chicken (about 2kg/4lb 4oz),
　cut into 6 pieces
4 tbsp brandy
1 fennel bulb, core removed
　and tender bulb thinly sliced
2 large onions, thinly sliced
2 garlic cloves, finely chopped
2–4 whole dried red or
　cayenne chillies
¼ cinnamon stick, broken
　into small pieces
¼ tsp ground or freshly
　grated nutmeg
½ tsp ground cardamom
3 carrots, cut diagonally into
　2.5cm (1in) thick slices
6 dried figs, halved
Grated zest of 1 lemon
300ml (11fl oz) chicken stock
6 strips preserved lemon,
　to garnish
Few leaves flat-leaf parsley,
　to garnish

Preheat the oven to 180°C (350°F), gas mark 4.

Heat half the olive oil in a large, heavy enamel or cast-iron casserole dish then fry the chicken pieces in batches for 2–3 minutes on each side, until brown all over. Transfer the chicken pieces to a plate and set aside.

Pour the brandy into the casserole dish to deglaze it, then pour the liquid over the chicken.

Heat the remaining olive oil in the casserole dish then add the fennel and onions and fry for 10–12 minutes, stirring gently, until nearly tender and slightly brown. Add the garlic, chillies and spices, then add the carrots, toss to coat and fry for a further 2–3 minutes. Add the figs and lemon zest, stir to combine then spread the vegetables into an even layer and place the browned chicken pieces on top, skin side up. Add chicken stock until it is 2.5cm (1in) deep. Reduce the heat, cover and simmer for 35–40 minutes, or alternatively, bring the stock back to the boil and place the dish in a 180°C (350°F), gas mark 4, oven for 45 minutes to 1 hour. Insert a meat thermometer into the thickest piece of chicken to check that the chicken is fully cooked – it should be 74°C (165°F).

Once the chicken is cooked, set the oven grill to hot and cook the chicken under the grill for 2–3 minutes to crisp up the skin. Remove from the grill, garnish with preserved lemon and serve.

Olive oil poaching is an extremely easy and forgiving cooking method. The fatal difficulty with fish is overcooking, which is nearly impossible to do here as the temperature is so low. This method produces sublime, tender, melt-in-the-mouth fish every time. It works with a range of fish, including less popular, less over-fished and difficult-to-cook varieties. These recipes highlight three of my favourite fish: yellowfin tuna, salmon and halibut.

OLIVE OIL POACHED SALMON WITH SPINACH

Serves 4

❦ ❦ ❦ ❦ ❦ ❦ ❦ ❦ ❦ ❦ ❦

4 salmon steaks of the same
    thickness (2.5–4cm/1–1½in),
    skin on (about 800g/
    1¾lb in total)
Coarse salt
1–2 litres (1¾–3½ pints)
    extra virgin olive oil
5 garlic cloves, peeled
    and cracked
1 whole dried red chilli
60g (2½oz) pine nuts, to serve
1 lemon, cut into 4 wedges,
    to serve

Spinach
2 tbsp extra virgin olive oil,
    plus extra for drizzling
2 garlic cloves, cut into thirds
800g (1¾lb) fresh spinach
80g (3¼oz) raisins
Salt and black pepper

Salt the salmon steaks on both sides, set them aside on a plate and leave them to cure for 30 minutes at room temperature.

Heat the olive oil a saucepan that will contain the fish in a single layer (packed tight is fine, but you don't want the steaks overlapping). Use a fryer thermometer to ensure it reaches 65°C (150°F) and maintains a consistent temperature. Add the garlic and chilli to the hot oil while the fish cures.

Brush any excess salt off the salmon steaks and place them gently in the oil. Ensure the oil temperature stays at around 63–68°C (145–155°F). Cook gently for 15–18 minutes until the salmon is firm to the touch and gives off tiny white beads of moisture.

While the salmon is poaching in the oil, cook the spinach. Heat the oil and garlic in a heavy-based frying pan over a medium heat for 3–4 minutes, then remove and discard the garlic. Add the spinach leaves to the pan in batches, a handful at a time, with a pinch of salt. Cook the spinach quickly, turning it with tongs and adding more spinach as the previous batch wilts. The pan should be hot enough that the water does not cook out of the spinach.

Once all the spinach leaves have been added, stir in the raisins and season with salt and pepper. Remove the salmon steaks from the oil and transfer to a plate lined with kitchen paper.

Divide the spinach among the plates, top with a salmon steak, drizzle with olive oil and sprinkle with the pine nuts. Serve with lemon wedges on the side.

❦ ❦ ❦

Tip: Fit the fish to the pan before heating the oil to ensure it fits in one layer without a lot of excess surrounding space. Change the width of the pan as necessary. Extra space costs more oil; a double layer prevents even cooking.

Halibut is another huge winner. The cherry tomatoes add a
bit of sparky acidity that cuts the richness of the oil-poached
fillet and brings the whole dish together.

HALIBUT WITH CHERRY TOMATOES

Serves 4

❧ ❧ ❧ ❧ ❧ ❧ ❧ ❧ ❧ ❧ ❧

4 halibut fillets of the same
   thickness (2.5–4cm/1–1½in),
   skin on (about 800g/1¾lb
   in total)
Coarse salt
1–2 litres (1¾–3½ pints) extra
   virgin olive oil
5 garlic cloves, peeled and
   cracked, plus 4 cloves, halved
1 whole dried red chilli
2 tbsp extra virgin olive oil
350g (12oz) cherry
   tomatoes, halved
Handful basil leaves, torn
Salt and black pepper

Salt the halibut fillets on both sides as on page 191.

Heat the olive oil in a saucepan as on page 191 and add the cracked garlic cloves and chilli to the hot oil while the fish cures.

Brush any excess salt off the halibut fillets and cook gently as before for 13–15 minutes, until the halibut is firm to the touch and gives off tiny white beads of moisture.

While the halibut is poaching, heat the 2 tablespoons of oil and the remaining garlic cloves in a heavy-based frying pan for 2 minutes, then remove and discard the garlic and reduce the heat to medium. Add the tomatoes to the pan and cook for 4–5 minutes, tossing occasionally, until the tomatoes have slightly caramelised, then add the basil and toss to combine. Remove from the heat, and transfer the halibut fillets to a plate lined with kitchen paper, skin side down.

Season the tomatoes with salt and pepper and serve immediately, alongside the halibut.

Here again, poaching in oil is the perfect cooking technique for yellowfin tuna – it softens the fish to silky smooth. I serve it with the salad niçoise combination of delicious homegrown boiled potatoes and green beans that we pick when small and tender. Blanching the beans in salt water preserves their vibrant green colour.

YELLOWFIN TUNA WITH GREEN BEANS AND POTATOES

Serves 4

❧ ❧ ❧ ❧ ❧ ❧ ❧ ❧ ❧ ❧

4 steaks yellowfin tuna
   of the same thickness
   (2.5–4cm/ 1–1½in), skin on
   (about 800g/ 1¾lb in total)
Coarse salt
400g (14oz) waxy potatoes,
   peeled
400g (14oz) green beans,
   topped and tailed
1–2 litres (1¾–3½ pints) extra
   virgin olive oil
5 garlic cloves, peeled and cracked
1 whole dried red chilli
Salt and black pepper
1 x quantity Caper Cream Sauce
   (see page 100), to serve
20g (¾oz) capers, to serve

Salt the tuna steaks on both sides as on page 191.

Meanwhile, place the potatoes in a large saucepan with a pinch of salt, fill with water to cover, place over a high heat and bring to the boil. Prepare a bowl of iced water. Once the water has reached the boil, reduce the heat to medium, add the green beans and cook for 6–8 minutes until *al dente*. When the beans are cooked, remove them from the water with tongs and plunge them into the iced water for 1–2 minutes to stop them cooking. Continue to cook the potatoes for a further 4–6 minutes, or until they are just tender when pierced with a sharp knife. Drain and allow to cool for 10 minutes.

Heat the olive oil in a saucepan as on page 191 and add the cracked garlic cloves and chilli to the hot oil while the fish cures.

Brush any excess salt off the tuna steaks and cook gently as before for 15–20 minutes, until the tuna is firm to the touch and gives off tiny white beads of moisture. Remove from the oil and transfer to a plate lined with kitchen paper.

Cut the cooled beans into 2cm (¾in) thick slices using an oiled knife. Toss the beans and potatoes together and season to taste with salt and pepper.

Serve the tuna with a dollop of caper cream sauce and a sprinkle of capers, with the beans and potatoes alongside.

Samfaina, Catalan ratatouille, uses roasted rather than raw peppers, as is common in other Mediterranean countries. This delicious variation adds a rich, silky sweetness to the dish. The recipe makes a large quantity, as I like to make two dishes from my *samfaina*, each with its own distinct culinary purpose. The first is the familiar vegetable side dish; the second requires cooking the *samfaina* down further, for a good hour or two, which transforms it into a fabulous jam-like sauce that is perfect paired with roasted or grilled fish, chicken and meat.

SAMFAINA

Serves 6 (with leftovers for making Samfaina jam)

❦ ❦ ❦ ❦ ❦ ❦ ❦ ❦ ❦ ❦ ❦

3 medium aubergines (about 700g/1½lb in total), cut into 1cm (½in) thick slices
80ml (3¼fl oz) extra virgin olive oil
1kg (2lb 2oz) sweet white onions, halved and thinly sliced
6 garlic cloves, finely chopped
2 small courgettes (about 350g/12oz in total), cubed
6 large oblong tomatoes (the Roma variety works well), peeled, deseeded and chopped
3 Roasted Red Peppers (see page 274), finely chopped
2–4 tbsp tomato paste
Pinch ground cinnamon
Large pinch cayenne pepper
Sherry vinegar, to taste
Salt and black pepper

Place the aubergine slices in a colander, sprinkle them with salt and set aside for 30 minutes, then wipe off the excess salt with kitchen paper and cut the slices into 2cm (¾in) cubes.

Heat the olive oil in a heavy-based casserole dish or cast-iron saucepan. Add the onions, garlic, cubed aubergine and courgette, and toss to coat. Reduce the heat to low, cover, and let the vegetables sweat for 10 minutes, then remove the lid, increase the heat to medium-high and cook until any excess liquid has evaporated.

Add the tomatoes, peppers, 2 tablespoons of the tomato paste, a pinch of salt and pepper, and the cinnamon and cayenne. Cook slowly over a low heat, uncovered, stirring occasionally, for 25–30 minutes. Taste and add another 1–2 tablespoons of tomato paste if desired. Continue cooking for a further 15–30 minutes, until it is a thick, rich stew. Add a splash of sherry vinegar to brighten the flavour and season to taste.

❦ ❦ ❦

Tip: Season the *samfaina* lightly and often throughout the cooking process. The flavours intensify as the *samfaina* reduces, and adding too much salt and pepper in one go early on can overwhelm rather than enhance the flavour of the vegetables.

This is a fantastic way to make *samfaina* into a vegetarian shared plate. The nuttiness of the chickpeas works beautifully with the sweet, rich vegetables and the creamy goat's cheese.

SAMFAINA WITH CHICKPEA CRÊPES, CRISPY CHICKPEAS AND GOAT'S CHEESE

Serves 4

❦ ❦ ❦ ❦ ❦ ❦ ❦ ❦ ❦ ❦ ❦

60g (2½oz) cooked chickpeas
  (see page 276 or use tinned)
60ml (2½fl oz) extra virgin
  olive oil
2 garlic cloves, bashed
Salt and black pepper

Crêpes
200g (7oz) chickpea flour
60ml (2½fl oz) extra virgin olive
  oil, plus extra for cooking
½ tsp salt flakes
½ tsp freshly ground
  black pepper
½ tsp ground cumin
½ tsp turmeric
¼ tsp cayenne pepper
Handful flat-leaf parsley,
  leaves finely chopped

Topping
300g (11oz) *Samfaina*
  (see page 195)
100g (3½oz) soft goat's cheese,
  broken into chunks
Finely sliced strips of peel
  from 1 lemon
Handful flat-leaf parsley, leaves
  roughly chopped

To peel the chickpeas, fill a large bowl with cold water. Add the cooked chickpeas to the water in batches and gently rub them for 5 minutes to remove the skins and excess starch (do this with tinned chickpeas, too, if using). Skim off the skins, drain the bowl, refill and repeat one or two times to remove all the skins. Drain, then make sure the chickpeas are completely dry.

Combine all the crêpe ingredients in a jug or bowl with 240ml (18½fl oz) water and whizz together with a hand-held blender. Add up to 120ml (4½fl oz) more water if needed, to achieve a thin batter.

Brush a heavy-based, non-stick frying pan or crêpe pan with olive oil and place over a high heat until very hot. Spoon in just enough batter to cover the base of the pan when swirled. Cook for 2–3 minutes then flip with a silicone spatula and cook for a further 2–3 minutes on the other side, until both sides are golden and crispy. Remove from the pan and continue cooking the crêpes until you have used up all the batter.

Heat the olive oil in a heavy-based frying pan and add the garlic. Cook the garlic until just brown, to flavour the oil, then remove and discard. Continue to heat the oil until it is very hot but not smoking. Add the chickpeas, shake to coat and fry for 5–6 minutes until golden and crunchy. Remove from the heat and season with salt and pepper.

Put a crêpe on a plate and cover half of it with a couple of heaped tablespoons of *samfaina*. Sprinkle over a few crispy chickpeas, spoon more *samfaina* over the top and garnish with goat's cheese, lemon peel, parsley and a few more chickpeas.

Our chickens give us fresh eggs every day, so eggs for dinner are a common occurrence at Can Riero. This is a delicious favourite – think autumnal carbonara. Ibiza's foraged revellon mushrooms are terrific here too, but any mix of wild mushrooms will do.

PASTA WITH EGG AND MUSHROOMS

Serves 4

❧ ❧ ❧ ❧ ❧ ❧ ❧ ❧ ❧ ❧ ❧

4 tbsp extra virgin olive oil
5 garlic cloves, peeled
    and cracked
Small sprig thyme, leaves
    finely chopped
Handful flat-leaf parsley,
    leaves finely chopped
200g (7oz) mixed wild
    mushrooms, cut into even
    bite-sized pieces
450g (1lb) pappardelle pasta
150g (5oz) cured pork belly, skin
    removed and meat cut into
    1cm (¾in) cubes or 150g (5oz)
    sliced Serrano ham, cut into
    1.5cm (¾in) ribbons
4 tbsp dry white wine
2 large eggs, plus 2 egg yolks
80g (3¼oz) Mahón curado or
    Pecorino cheese, grated

Heat half the olive oil in a heavy-based frying pan over a medium-high heat. Add 1 garlic clove, cook it for 3–4 minutes, then remove and discard. Add the thyme leaves and half the parsley to the pan and shake to mix, then add the mushrooms, adding the densest first, and cook for 2–3 minutes, tossing occasionally. Remove the mushrooms and herbs from the pan and set aside.

Cook the pasta according to the packet instructions, then drain, reserving the cooking water.

Heat the remaining olive oil in the frying pan over a medium-high heat, add the remaining garlic cloves and cook for 6–7 minutes until brown, then remove and discard. Add the pork belly to the pan and cook for 4–5 minutes until brown on all sides, or if using Serrano ham cook for 2–3 minutes. Pour in the wine and cook for a further 6–8 minutes, until it has reduced. Add 4 tablespoons of the pasta water (the starch is essential, so tap water doesn't work here) and the cooked pasta. Shake the pan to combine.

Meanwhile, whisk together the eggs and egg yolks in a bowl. Slowly pour 120ml (4½fl oz) of the hot pasta water into the egg mixture to temper the eggs. Remove the pasta from the heat and add the tempered eggs very slowly, tossing the pasta gently with silicone-tipped tongs – you don't want the eggs to scramble. Add 60g (2½oz) of the cheese and season with salt and pepper. Stir to combine and taste.

Make a nest of pasta on each plate, top it with the mushrooms and sprinkle with the remaining grated cheese and parsley.

❧ ❧ ❧

Tip: Try to get as many shapes and sizes of mushrooms as possible; it makes the dish much more interesting. Avoid common button mushrooms as they have more water and less flavour, but if they are all that are available they too can be made delicious with a bit of extra cooking. First, sauté them with the thyme, a pinch of salt, pepper and olive oil for 10-15 minutes until they are completely dry, then enhance the flavour by adding a splash of white wine and cooking them again until dry.

This unique recipe is adapted from Ibiza friends John and Jane Veale, both excellent cooks and fabulous hosts. I have had an Italian or two regard me with utter disdain at the idea of pasta paired with fresh fig and chilli, only to be bowled over with its deliciousness. An unusual combination, but there is something very special about the the rich sweetness of the fig, the heat of the chilli and the bite of the pasta. It is an early autumn staple and one of our most-requested dishes at Can Riero. It is truly an inspired innovation.

FIG PASTA

Serves 4

❦ ❦ ❦ ❦ ❦ ❦ ❦ ❦ ❦ ❦ ❦

500g (1lb 2oz) spaghetti
   or pappardelle pasta
60ml (2½fl oz) double cream
2 rosemary sprigs
6 thyme sprigs
2 tbsp extra virgin olive oil
12 fresh black figs, cut into
   eighths
2 small dried red chillies,
   deseeded and finely chopped
Finely grated zest of 2 lemons
50g (2oz) Mahón curado or
   Parmesan cheese, finely grated
Salt and black pepper

Cook the pasta according to the packet instructions, then drain and set aside.

Put the cream, rosemary and thyme in a small saucepan and bring to the boil. Remove the pan from the heat and set aside to infuse for 30 minutes.

Heat the olive oil in a large frying pan until hot, then add the figs and chillies and cook for 2–3 minutes until the figs caramelise, shaking the pan vigorously every few seconds. The figs should be intact and not mushy.

Strain the infused cream through a fine-mesh sieve into a bowl and discard the herbs. Add the lemon zest to the cream, pour the cream over the figs and shake the pan to heat through.

Combine the pasta and 40g (1½oz) of the grated cheese with the cream and figs. Season to taste, then sprinkle with the remaining cheese and serve.

This savoury shared plate and the following roasted fig dessert are wonderful dishes – simple, elegant and just delicious. They are fantastic for those without a fig tree in the garden, as roasting really enhances the flavour. Figs are proof that a few great ingredients can add up to an astonishing bite. The classic flavour combination of blue cheese, walnut and fig is just that.

FIGS WITH QUESO AZUL AND CANDIED WALNUTS

Makes 6 stuffed figs

✦ ✦ ✦ ✦ ✦ ✦ ✦ ✦ ✦ ✦ ✦

6 fresh, ripe green or black figs
3 tbsp crème fraîche
300g (11oz) *queso azul*
   (Spanish blue cheese)

Candied walnuts
2 tbsp butter
70g (3oz) soft light brown sugar
Large pinch cayenne pepper
Large pinch salt
60g (2½oz) walnuts

Preheat the oven to 180°C (350°F), gas mark 4 and line a baking tray with baking parchment.

To make the candied walnuts, place the butter, sugar, cayenne pepper and salt in a saucepan over a medium heat and stir until the butter has melted. Add the walnuts to the pan and stir to coat completely. Stir continuously over the heat for 4–5 minutes, until the nuts are evenly coated and the sugar mixture darkens and caramelises. Be careful not to burn the nuts or the sugar. Transfer the candied nuts to the lined tray, break up any clumps with a wooden spoon and leave to cool.

Cut a deep cross in the top of each fig and pinch from the bottom to open. Stuff each fig with half a tablespoon of crème fraîche then stuff each with 50g (2oz) blue cheese. Place the figs in a roasting tin and bake for 6–8 minutes, or until the cheese has melted and the figs are slightly gooey. Remove, sprinkle with candied walnuts, and serve immediately.

Green and black figs ripen in Ibiza's late summer and early autumn. An integral part of *campo* life, they are delicious fresh off the tree. We also like them stuffed with Pata Negra ham or black pepper and ricotta, baked with cinnamon and honey, or grilled and served with cinnamon ice cream. Traditionally, farmers dry figs on rooftops on a bed of pine needles and the fruits, stuffed with almonds, are eaten throughout the year. Catalina, the mother of my friend Vicente, the beekeeper, gave me my first almond-stuffed fig a few autumns ago. The figs had been dried in the traditional way and the almonds had been gathered and left to sun roast before being cracked. No bite is closer to the heart of the Ibiza countryside.

DRIED FIGS STUFFED WITH ALMONDS
Makes 12 stuffed figs

❧ ❧ ❧ ❧ ❧ ❧ ❧ ❧ ❧ ❧ ❧

12 large whole dried figs
24 whole blanched
    toasted almonds

Slice into the side of each fig, stuff each fig with 2 almonds, then press it closed.

❧ ❧ ❧

Tips: Don't be tempted by early-season or underripe fruit. If the figs are on the wrong side of delicious, quarter them lengthways, cutting halfway down the fruit and leaving the bottom intact. Open slightly, spray inside with a good balsamic vinegar and roast in a medium hot oven for 10 minutes to enhance the flavour.

Dip a cotton bud in olive oil and dab the bottom of unripe figs, still attached to the tree, to hasten tree-ripening. A harvest-sized fig dabbed with olive oil will ripen overnight. Figs usually ripen all at once – use this tip to extend the season or to rescue a crop before it rains.

This is a wonderful dessert: the honey, figs and oranges all come from the farm, making it easy for me to throw this together. We use ice cream that is handmade by Benvenuto and Monica at Zero Gradi, in Santa Gertrudis. I always have some cinnamon ice cream on hand; it is beyond a doubt my favourite flavour.

ORANGE AND HONEY CARAMELISED FIGS

Serves 4

❧ ❧ ❧ ❧ ❧ ❧ ❧ ❧ ❧ ❧

3 tbsp runny honey
½ tsp ground cinnamon
Grated zest of ½ orange,
    plus the juice (if needed)
¼ tsp coarse salt
8 fresh, ripe black or
    green figs, halved
Cinnamon ice cream,
    to serve

Preheat the oven to 180°C (350°F), gas mark 4.

Combine the honey, cinnamon, orange zest and salt together in a bowl.

Cut the figs in half widthways and arrange them on a baking tray, cut sides up.

If the figs are dry, squeeze a little orange juice over them. Drizzle the honey mixture over the figs with a spoon and bake them for 8–10 minutes, until the figs are gooey. Remove from the oven, allow to cool until just warm, then serve with cinnamon ice cream.

❧ ❧ ❧

Tip: The important bit is getting the best-quality ice cream possible. Vanilla works well if cinnamon is unavailable.

Café con leche, the iconic Spanish coffee with milk, translates beautifully into a retro roulade. The flavours are an exquisite, simple alliance, like the drink itself. Light chocolate deepened with brandy, pure unflavoured whipped cream and coffee glaze: nothing could be more delicious or more authentic. The sponge is based on Rose Beranbaum's biscuit recipe. It is similar to the sponge used in France as a base for fancy pastries. There is no better cake to roll: it doesn't crack or tear, and it absorbs the syrup without getting spongy. It can also be made up to 24 hours ahead of serving.

CAFÉ CON LECHE ROULADE

Serves 10–12

❧ ❧ ❧ ❧ ❧ ❧ ❧ ❧ ❧ ❧ ❧

You will need: 39 x 24cm (15 x 9½in) rectangular cake tin or Swiss roll tin

Butter, for greasing
4 large eggs, plus 1 large egg yolk, at room temperature
125g (4½oz) caster sugar
30g (1¼oz) cocoa powder
4½ tbsp boiling water
1½ tsp brandy
50g (2oz) plain flour, sifted, plus extra for dusting
1 x quantity Stabilised Whipped Cream (see page 286)
100g (3½oz) good-quality milk chocolate, melted, to drizzle
75g (3oz) chopped walnuts, toasted, to garnish

Soaking syrup
30g (1¼oz) caster sugar
1½ tbsp Mallorcan Café Rico, coffee liqueur or Kahlúa

Coffee glaze
1 tsp lemon juice
1½ tbsp strong freshly made espresso
100g (3½oz) icing sugar

Position the oven rack in the lower third of the oven and preheat the oven to 220°C (430°F), gas mark 7.

Grease the tin with butter and line the base and sides with baking parchment, making sure it comes right up the sides and just above the top edge of the tin on all sides. Grease the paper with butter and dust with flour. Set aside.

To make the sponge base, separate 2 of the eggs, placing the yolks in a mixing bowl or the bowl of a stand mixer with the extra yolk, setting aside the whites in a separate, clean bowl. Add the 2 remaining eggs and the sugar to the bowl with the egg yolks and beat at high speed or with a hand-held electric whisk for 5 minutes, or until pale and very thick. The volume should more than double and when the whisk is lifted the mixture should leave a ribbon trail in the bowl.

Dissolve the cocoa powder in the boiling water, stirring with a fork to break up any lumps, then add the brandy and whisk until smooth. With the mixer or whisk at low speed, pour the cocoa powder mixture down the side of the bowl and beat until just incorporated. Remove the whisk from the bowl and sift half the flour over the egg mixture, folding it in gently but quickly with a large flat rubber spatula until well incorporated. Sift the remaining flour over the batter and fold it in. Transfer the sponge mixture to another large bowl and set aside.

Thoroughly clean and dry the stand mixer bowl or mixing bowl and the whisk, reassemble and add the egg whites to the bowl. Beat the egg whites at medium speed until foamy, then increase the speed and beat for about 2 minutes, until stiff peaks form when the whisk is lifted.

Recipe continued overleaf

Fold the egg whites gently into the sponge mixture, in 2 separate additions, then pour the mixture into the prepared tin and level it out with an angled metal spatula. Pick up the tin and drop it squarely on to the work surface – this will remove any bubbles that form as the batter is poured in.

Bake for 8–9 minutes, or until golden, and a toothpick inserted into the sponge comes out clean and the cake is springy to the touch. Remove from the oven, loosen the cake from the edges of the tin with a knife, and cover the tin tightly with a clean cotton kitchen towel. Flip the cake over onto the work surface, baking parchment side up. Roll the cake lengthways, paper inside, cloth outside. Roll the cake tightly, then set aside to cool, seam side down, on a wire rack. Rolling the cake while warm is essential for keeping the shape of the finished roulade. Leave to completely cool for a few hours or overnight.

To make the soaking syrup, place the sugar and 4 tablespoons of water in a small saucepan and bring to a rolling boil, stirring constantly. Add the coffee liqueur, stir to combine and set aside. When cool, transfer to a small jar with a lid. The syrup can be made a day or two in advance.

To make the coffee glaze, combine the lemon juice and coffee in a small bowl and add half of the icing sugar. Whisk until the sugar is thoroughly combined and the mixture is smooth, then add the remaining sugar and whisk again to incorporate. The texture of the glaze should be loose enough to drizzle, but thick enough to stay in place. If it is too thick to drizzle, add a bit more coffee or lemon juice. If it is too thin, add another tablespoon of icing sugar.

To assemble, unroll the towel-wrapped cake and carefully peel off the baking parchment. Poke tiny holes all over the cake, to about one-quarter of its depth, on the side where the paper was removed, and paint the cake with the cooled syrup using a pastry brush. Spread whipped cream evenly over the top, leaving a 2.5cm (1in) gap of uncovered sponge at one end to prevent overspill.

Roll the sponge as before, taking care not to squish out the cream, then plate it seam side down on a serving dish. Drizzle the roulade generously with coffee glaze, drizzle over the melted chocolate and sprinkle with toasted walnuts to serve.

Truffles are truly decadent. We like milk chocolate in combination with
mandarin peel and 100 per cent cocoa powder; it gives a slight bitter edge
to the outside of these truffles, and a sweet, spiced, creamy inside.

SPICED CHOCOLATE TRUFFLES

Makes 20 truffles

❦ ❦ ❦ ❦ ❦ ❦ ❦ ❦ ❦ ❦ ❦

1 whole nutmeg
100ml (3½fl oz) double cream
Pared strips of peel from
   1 mandarin
Large pinch salt
½ cinnamon stick, halved
6 whole cloves
250g (9oz) best-quality milk
   chocolate, roughly chopped
100g (3½oz) Dutch process
   100 per cent cocoa powder
   (or other good-quality
   cocoa powder)

Put the nutmeg in a plastic bag and smash it with a rolling pin
until it breaks into 2–3 chunks.

Put the cream, nutmeg chunks, mandarin peel, salt, cinnamon
and cloves in a small saucepan and heat gently until it nearly
reaches the boil. Remove the pan from the heat and set aside to
steep for 1 hour, then reheat until it nearly reaches the boil and
strain through a fine-mesh sieve into a heatproof bowl,
discarding the spices and mandarin peel.

Place the chopped chocolate in a separate, small heatproof
bowl and pour over the hot cream. Stir until the chocolate has
melted and is completely incorporated with the cream, then
let the mixture cool a little, cover the bowl with clingfilm and
transfer to the fridge for 1 hour, or until firm.

Scrape the chocolate truffle mixture onto a clean work
surface, roll it into a log about 3cm (1¼in) in diameter then
press the log to form an oblong. Heat the blade of a sharp knife
in hot water, dry the blade then cut the chocolate into bite-sized
squares. Spread the cocoa powder on a large plate and dredge
the chocolate squares in the powder to coat. The truffles will
keep in a cool, dry place for up to 2 days.

❦ ❦ ❦

Tip: Steeping the spices in the cream for one hour is important
as it imparts the flavour of the spices, which is crucial to the
finished truffles.

WINTER

Winter on Ibiza is heavenly and brief, really just January and February. The island is quiet and still, as if in hibernation. The landscape is brilliant green and scented by wet pines. The weather is humid and cold – the kind that cuts, that you need to dress for – and punctuated with occasional ferocious downpours that feel like a power above has opened a tap that pours over us in a thick, steady stream. We get winds, too, sometimes; winds that bend our palm trees and roil the sea, making it impossible for the ferries to get across. As our local shops run short on supplies we are reminded that Ibiza is an island in the storm-tossed winter Mediterranean.

Our favourite way to spend a Sunday is taking a long walk on the beach with family and friends on a crisp, sunny day, followed by a rich, comforting meal in front of the fire. Spinach, foraged and cultivated, is a staple of the season, along with pumpkin, broccoli, carrots, sweet potatoes, potatoes, cauliflower and onions. We use lots of what we prepared in the autumn, too – tomatoes roasted or made into sauce, or roasted red pepper sauce – to create slow-cooked stews, soups, braises and roasts. We cook with what we have preserved or dried as well: borlotti beans, broad beans, chutneys and pickles. All these ingredients fill the farmhouse with the scents of glorious, gently bubbling meals accented with citrus, warming spices and smoky Pimentón de la Vera.

These stuffed mussels were inspired by a long-ago romantic New England seaside dinner with my now husband Rene. Like many of my recipes, it has been adapted to use Mediterranean ingredients found on Ibiza. The combination of brandy, almonds and mussels is genius: local food at its finest.

STUFFED MUSSELS WITH BRANDY AND ALMONDS

Serves 4 as a starter

✦ ✦ ✦ ✦ ✦ ✦ ✦ ✦ ✦ ✦ ✦

240ml (8½fl oz) white wine
24 mussels, cleaned and
   debearded (see page 75)
60g (2½oz) toasted blanched
   almonds
50g (2oz) breadcrumbs
2 tbsp extra virgin olive oil
2 garlic cloves, finely chopped
1 dried red chilli, deseeded
   and finely chopped
25g (1oz) butter, softened
Finely grated zest of 1 lemon
Small handful flat-leaf parsley,
   leaves roughly chopped
2 tbsp brandy
Salt and black pepper

Bring the wine to the boil in a heavy-based saucepan over a high heat then add the mussels, shake well, and cover the pan tightly. Cook the mussels for 5–6 minutes until the mussels are open.

Remove the pan from the heat, and tip the mussels into a dish. Discard any that are still closed and set the rest aside to cool.

Place the almonds and breadcrumbs in the bowl of a food processor and blitz to make a fine crumb.

Heat the olive oil in a heavy-based frying pan, add the garlic and chilli and fry for 3-4 minutes, then add the almond–breadcrumb mixture and fry for a further 6–8 minutes, until the crumbs are crisp and golden. Remove from the heat and add the butter, lemon zest, parsley and brandy. Mix well to combine and season with salt and pepper.

Open and detach the mussels, leaving them on a half shell. Stuff the mussel shells with the seasoned crumb mixture then place them on a baking tray. Lightly drizzle with olive oil to encourage browning. Preheat the grill to medium.

Grill them for 5–7 minutes under the grill until golden and serve on the half shell.

We plant an abundance of broad beans every autumn and early spring. They are an amazing ingredient and a great organic fertiliser, feeding nitrogen back into the soil. What we can't eat fresh we sun-dry, preserving young green beans for use during winter. Most shop-bought dried broad beans are yellow, signifying that they are mature beans. If you can't find small, green dried broad beans, use chickpeas instead. Falafel is a great make-ahead meal. Shape the uncooked batter and freeze until needed.

DRIED BROAD BEAN FALAFEL

Serves 4 (makes 12–16 falafel)

❦ ❦ ❦ ❦ ❦ ❦ ❦ ❦ ❦ ❦ ❦

300g (11oz) dried baby broad beans, or chickpeas, soaked overnight in cold water
¼ sweet onion, grated and pressed dry with kitchen towel
3 garlic cloves, crushed
Handful coriander, leaves chopped
Handful flat-leaf parsley, leaves chopped
1 tsp ground cumin
1 tsp ground coriander
⅛ tsp ground cinnamon
¼ tsp ground or freshly grated nutmeg
½ tsp cayenne pepper
4 tbsp tahini
350–500ml (12–18fl oz) extra virgin olive oil, for frying
Salt and black pepper
Pita Bread (see page 292), Hummus (see page 276), Carrot and Red Cabbage Slaw (see page 291), yoghurt, Cucumber and Onion Pickles (see page 277) and hot sauce, to serve

Drain the beans or chickpeas and place them in the bowl of a food processor with the onion and garlic and whizz until the mixture comes together but is still slightly lumpy. Add the herbs and pulse to combine, until the mixture has a green tinge, then add the spices and tahini and pulse until well combined yet still coarsely textured. Tip the mixture into a bowl, bring it together with your hands, then cover the bowl with clingfilm and chill for 20 minutes.

Pour olive oil into a deep saucepan until it is 6cm (2½in) deep (the quantity will depend on the size of the pan) and heat to 185°C (365°F). Shape the chilled falafel mixture into 12 medium or 16 small quenelles or balls. Drop the falafel carefully into the oil and fry for 4–5 minutes, rolling them once or twice, until they are brown and crispy. Use a spider or slotted spoon to remove them from the hot oil and transfer to a plate lined with kitchen paper.

Serve immediately with pita bread, hummus, carrot and red cabbage slaw, cucumber and onion pickles and hot sauce.

To shape quenelles
Hold two clean tablespoons in your hands, with the points facing each other and the bowls of each spoon facing you. Scoop up a half to two-thirds of a tablespoon of the falafel mixture with the left-hand spoon. With the right-hand spoon 'slice' up and over the mixture, compressing and scraping the bowl of the right-hand spoon on the top edge of the left spoon to transfer the mixture to the right-hand spoon. Bring the right-hand spoon around the back of the left and 'slice' down, scraping the top of the right-hand spoon against the bottom of the left-hand spoon to transfer the mixture back. Repeat several times to compress the falafel into a firm, three-sided rugby ball shapes.

Ibiza sweet potatoes are extremely popular from late autumn throughout the winter; market stalls are overflowing with them. Here they are paired with evaporated milk for an incredibly warm and silky soup. It tastes like I imagine Ibiza smelled when the Moors ruled. Perfect after a long Sunday walk through the old Moorish settlement overlooking the Sant Mateu Valley.

SILKY SWEET POTATO SOUP

Serves 6

❦ ❦ ❦ ❦ ❦ ❦ ❦ ❦ ❦ ❦ ❦

500g (1lb 2oz) butternut squash, deseeded and cut into 1.5cm (⅔in) dice
4 carrots, cut into 4cm (2in) long sticks
3 tbsp extra virgin olive oil, plus extra for roasting
2 large onions, cut into 1.5cm (⅔in) thick slices
1kg (2lb 2oz) sweet potatoes, pierced all over
6 garlic cloves, finely chopped
¼ tsp cayenne pepper
¼ tsp turmeric
¼ tsp ground cumin
¼ tsp ground cinnamon
1 large pinch ground or freshly grated nutmeg
400ml (14fl oz) evaporated milk
1.5 litres (2½ pints) vegetable stock
Splash aged sherry vinegar
120ml (4½fl oz) goat's milk yoghurt (or regular cow's milk yoghurt)
40g (1½oz) pine nuts, toasted
Salt and black pepper

Preheat the oven to 180°C (350°F), gas mark 4.

Put the butternut squash and carrots on a baking tray, toss with olive oil to coat, and sprinkle with salt and pepper. Put the sliced onions on a separate baking tray and do the same. Wrap the sweet potatoes in foil and place them in the oven.

Roast the vegetables until they are soft and golden: the carrots and squash will take 20–30 minutes; the onions 30–40 minutes; and the whole sweet potatoes 40–50 minutes. Remove from the oven, allow to cool, and remove any charred bits. Peel the squash and sweet potatoes, combine the vegetables in a bowl and set aside.

Heat the olive oil in a heavy-based saucepan, then add the garlic and spices and fry for 5–6 minutes. Add the roasted vegetables, stir to combine and cook for a further 3–4 minutes. Add the evaporated milk and bring to a simmer. Cook for 5 minutes, then add the stock, return to a simmer and purée with a hand-held blender.

Cook the soup, uncovered, for 30 minutes over a very low heat (use a heat diffuser or flame tamer if you have one) then season to taste and add a splash of vinegar. Drizzle with yoghurt, sprinkle with pine nuts and a crack of black pepper and serve.

❦ ❦ ❦

Tip: For a silky smooth consistency, pass the soup through a sieve, discarding any vegetable purée left in the sieve.

Wild spinach is prolific all over the *campo* from the first heavy, cold, late-autumn rain right through to late spring. We have so much growing on the farm that we feed baskets of it to the chickens every couple of days, complete with snails. The beauty is that it grows right back. This is a great basic soup for any strong leafy green; vary it using Swiss chard or kale.

WILD SPINACH SOUP WITH GARLIC CROUTONS

Serves 4–6, with leftovers

❦ ❦ ❦ ❦ ❦ ❦ ❦ ❦ ❦ ❦

2 tbsp extra virgin olive oil
750g (1lb 10oz) onions, cut into
    0.5cm (⅛ in) thick slices
2 pinches brown sugar (optional)
1.5kg (3lb 4oz) spinach
    leaves, cleaned
1 tsp salt
¾ tsp freshly ground
    black pepper
1.5 litres (2½ pints)
    vegetable stock
1 tbsp lemon juice
2 tbsp crème fraîche
Salt and black pepper

Garlic croutons
4 tbsp extra virgin olive oil
2 garlic cloves, bashed
½ ciabatta or baguette,
    cut into 2cm (¾in) cubes
½ tsp salt flakes

Heat the olive oil in a large, heavy-based saucepan over a low heat. Add the onions and a pinch of salt and fry, stirring, over a very low heat for 15 minutes. Taste and add the brown sugar, if desired, then continue to cook gently, uncovered, for 30–45 minutes, until the onions are almost disintegrating.

Put the clean spinach in a colander in the kitchen sink and boil a full kettle of water. Pour the boiling water over the spinach slowly, turning the leaves with tongs so they are evenly exposed to the hot water, and leave to wilt. Add the spinach to the slow-cooked onions along with the salt and pepper. Stir to combine, then add enough stock to fill the pan to 1cm (½in) above the vegetables. Bring to a simmer and cook for 10–12 minutes to marry the flavours, then remove from the heat, purée with a hand-held blender until smooth and season with lemon juice and more salt and pepper, if necessary.

To make the croutons, heat the olive oil and garlic in a frying pan over a medium heat. Fry for 5 minutes then remove and discard the garlic. Add the bread and fry for 4–5 minutes, tossing every now and again. Sprinkle with salt flakes. Swirl the crème fraîche into the soup and scatter over the croutons to serve.

❦ ❦ ❦

Tip: Our food stylist, Lizzie, an incredible cook, came up with this technique to wilt spinach. It saves time and the leaves stay a gorgeous bright green. Use this method in any spinach recipe.

This pumpkin soup recipe is similar to the spinach version in that it begins with an onion *sofregit*, but this one is great for squash and root vegetables. Carrot is essential here, as it adds a delicate sweetness. I like to finish the soup with a good aged sherry vinegar which perfectly matches the pumpkin.

PUMPKIN SOUP WITH SAGE OIL

Serves 4, with leftovers

2 tbsp extra virgin olive oil
750g (1lb 10oz) onions, cut
    into 0.5cm (¼in) thick slices
2 pinches soft brown sugar
    (optional)
750g (1lb 10oz) pumpkin, peeled,
    deseeded and roughly chopped
300g carrots (11 oz), peeled
    and sliced
1½ litres (2½ pints) chicken
    or vegetable stock
Pinch ground or freshly
    grated nutmeg
1–2 tsp aged sherry vinegar
Salt and black pepper

Sage oil
2 handfuls sage leaves,
    veins removed
3 tbsp extra virgin olive oil
Splash Habanero Hot Sauce
    (see page 284)
½ tsp salt
½ tsp freshly ground black pepper

To make the sage oil, put all the ingredients in a cylindrical container and purée with a hand-held blender until smooth. Set aside at room temperature for 30 minutes or more to infuse the flavours.

Heat the olive oil in a large, heavy-based saucepan over a low heat. Add the onions and a pinch of salt and fry, stirring, over a very low heat for 15 minutes. Taste and add a little brown sugar, if desired, then continue to cook gently, uncovered, for 30–45 minutes, until the onions are almost falling apart.

Add the pumpkin and carrots, fry for 3–4 minutes, stirring the pumpkin into the onions, then add the stock and nutmeg and season with salt and pepper. Bring to a simmer, stirring to scrape the onion from the bottom of the pan, and simmer for 15–20 minutes, or until the pumpkin is tender. Remove from the heat, use a hand-held blender to purée the soup until smooth. Add more stock if the soup is too thick.

Taste and season with salt, pepper and vinegar. Serve drizzled with the sage oil.

Carne picada means ground meat, or mince. It is an incredible, versatile and economic beginning for many fabulous recipes. My wonderful butcher Emilio grinds it for me to order at Carniceria Pepita y Emilio, in the Santa Eulària Market. The meat is typically 10 per cent fat, which is perfect: fairly lean, but with enough fat for flavour and moisture. This is great for *albóndigas* or *rollo de carne*, or even as a burger mix. Make it fancy with the roasted pepper, goat's cheese and pine nut layer in the middle or, if time is short, skip the layering and serve with Roasted Red Pepper Sauce (see page 283) on the side, topped with goat's cheese and a sprinkle of pine nuts. It's delicious whatever the choice.

BEEF AND CHORIZO ROLLO DE CARNE

Serves 6, with leftovers

✦ ✦ ✦ ✦ ✦ ✦ ✦ ✦ ✦ ✦ ✦

4 tbsp extra virgin olive oil
225g (8oz) chestnut or baby portobello mushrooms, thickly sliced
1 large sweet onion, finely chopped
4 large garlic cloves, finely chopped
1 tbsp tomato paste
120ml (4½fl oz) chicken stock
5 tbsp sherry
1 tbsp anchovy paste
4–6 slices day-old white bread, crumbled, or ready-made breadcrumbs (90–120g/ 3½–4½oz)
2 large eggs
2 tsp thyme leaves
1½ tsp salt
¾ tsp freshly ground black pepper
1 tsp pimentón dulce (sweet paprika)
⅛ tsp ground coriander
Small handful flat-leaf parsley leaves
60–120ml (2½–4½fl oz) whole milk
150g (5oz) picante (hot) chorizo, skin removed and meat crumbled
850g (1¾lb) minced beef (10 per cent fat)
4–6 Roasted Tomatoes (see page 275)
1 tbsp soft light brown sugar

Preheat the oven to 180°C (350°F), gas mark 4.

Heat 2 tablespoons of the olive oil in a heavy-based saucepan over a medium-high heat, add the mushrooms and onion and fry for 5–7 minutes, until they begin to brown. Add the garlic and fry for 5–6 minutes, until lightly coloured, then stir in the tomato paste and cook for a further 2–3 minutes. Add 75ml (3fl oz) of the chicken stock and 3 tablespoons of the sherry. Cook for 4–5 minutes until the mixture starts to thicken, then stir in the anchovy paste and cook for 1–2 minutes. Remove the mixture from the heat, transfer to a large heatproof bowl and set aside.

Deglaze the saucepan with the remaining sherry, scraping up any bits that have stuck to the bottom of the pan, simmer for 3–5 minutes, then add the liquid to the bowl containing the mushroom mixture and leave to cool to room temperature.

When cool, add the breadcrumbs, eggs, herbs and spices to the vegetable mix to form a stiff mixture. Add 60ml (2½fl oz) of the milk and incorporate, adding more milk as needed, until the mixture is moist and still quite stiff. Add the chorizo and minced beef to the mixture and combine.

Wrap a cooling rack in foil, poke holes in the foil to drain the fat and place the foil-wrapped rack in a baking tray.

To make the stuffing, line up the roasted red pepper quarters lengthways on a piece of baking paper so that they are touching each other. Place the goat's cheese rounds down the middle of the row of peppers across the row, so each

Recipe continued overleaf

Goat's cheese and pepper stuffing
5 Roasted Red Peppers
   (see page 274)
225g (8oz) mild creamy goat's
   cheese, frozen until firm,
   then sliced into 1cm (½in)
   thick rounds
75g (3oz) toasted pine nuts

To make albóndigas
30g (1¼oz) toasted pine nuts
100g (3½oz) creamy mild
   goat's cheese

pepper quarter has a round of goat's cheese on it. Sprinkle the pine nuts over the cheese then roll up the pepper quarters tightly, to enclose the goat's cheese.

Divide the meat mixture in half. On the foil-covered rack, shape one half into a rectangle 5cm (2in) longer than the goat's cheese and pepper roll. Press the pepper and cheese roll into the meat base. Shape the remaining meat into a rectangle of equal length, but slightly wider. Place it on top of the bottom half and pat and press all the way around to seal the rollo.

Place the roasted tomatoes lengthways on the rollo de carne, running along the top from one end to the other. Drizzle with 2 tablespoons of the olive oil and sprinkle with sugar, salt and pepper. Transfer the rollo to the oven and bake for 1 hour 10 minutes–1 hour 15 minutes, until crispy and browned. To ensure it is completely cooked, insert a meat thermometer into the meat – it should read 71°C (160°F).

🌱 🌱 🌱

Tip: If you prefer, you can make this mix into *albóndigas*, or meatballs. Shape the mixture into balls about the size of a walnut. Poke a hole halfway into each ball, stuff with a bit of goat's cheese and pinch shut. Place the meatballs on a baking tray and cook under a hot grill for 10–15 minutes, turning them occasionally, until browned all over and firm to the touch, then transfer to a serving dish, drizzle with Roasted Tomato Sauce (see page 282) and sprinkle with the remaining goat's cheese. Grill for 3–5 minutes to melt the cheese.

Bocadillos are eaten everywhere; from not-very-exciting ones in airports, to fancier bakery versions, to the more imaginative ones found in tapas bars. On Ibiza they usually involve ham, sliced chorizo, cheese, a combination thereof, or tortilla. We like ours like a small meal served on gorgeous bread. This *bocadillo* definitely qualifies: dripping with sauce, stuffed with goat's cheese and veg – the perfect reason to make extra meatballs.

BOCADILLO DE ALBÓNDIGAS

Serves 4

❦ ❦ ❦ ❦ ❦ ❦ ❦ ❦ ❦ ❦ ❦ ❦

4 sandwich rolls
Extra virgin olive oil,
    for brushing
20 *albóndigas* (see page 226)
1 Roasted Red Pepper
    (see page 274), shredded
80g (3¼oz) soft goat's cheese
Large handful baby spinach
    leaves
120g (4½oz) Roasted Red Pepper
    Sauce (see page 283),
    plus extra for dipping
Salt and black pepper

Slice the rolls in half lengthways and brush both cut sides with olive oil. Grill the halved rolls under a medium grill, cut side up, until warmed through and lightly toasted. Remove from the grill.

Layer on all the ingredients, drizzle the roasted red pepper sauce over the top and season with salt and pepper. Serve with a bowl of roasted red pepper sauce for dipping.

❦ ❦ ❦

Tip: Albóndigas are a great main ingredient with a variety of sandwich fillings. Try them in toasted pita bread (see page 292) with melted Manchego semi-curado, caramelised onions and roasted tomato sauce.

This *guisado* made with both types of Pimentón de la Vera – sweet (*dulce*) and spicy (*picante*) – was my first foray into applying the new ingredients I encountered on Ibiza to a recipe I grew up with. Pimentón originated in the Americas and was brought to Spain by early explorers. Pimentón de La Vera, like Pata Negra ham or Mahón cheese, has Protected Designation of Origin (PDO) status, meaning it can only come from a specific region, in this case Extremadura. The peppers are air-dried and oak-smoked until dry, then stone-ground. The flavour is aromatic, rich and slightly smoky, whether hot or sweet. It makes wonderful *guisado* and is not difficult to find.

BEEF AND BEAN GUISADO

Serves 6

4 tbsp extra virgin olive oil
1kg (2lb 2oz) onions,
    finely chopped
5 garlic cloves, finely chopped
3 tbsp pimentón dulce
    (sweet paprika)
2 tbsp pimentón picante
    (hot paprika)
¼ tsp cayenne pepper
¼ tsp ground cumin
¼ tsp ground coriander
750g (1lb 10oz) minced beef
    (15 per cent fat)
3 Roasted Red Peppers (see
    page 274), deseeded and
    roughly chopped
750g (1lb 10oz) Grated Tomatoes
    (see page 275) or 2 x 400g
    (14oz) tins chopped tomatoes
800g (1¾lb) cooked pinto beans
    (see page 276), drained
4 tbsp tomato paste
½ tsp dried thyme
1 dried bay leaf
Salt and black pepper

Heat half the olive oil in a large, heavy-based frying pan over a medium-high heat and add the onions and garlic. Fry for 10–12 minutes until soft but not browned, then add the spices, stir and continue to fry for a further 5–8 minutes until lightly browned and fragrant, then remove from the heat to a bowl.

Heat the remaining olive oil in the frying pan and fry the minced beef for 6–8 minutes, until browned, breaking up the mince with a wooden spoon. Drain away the fat and add the onions and garlic to the pan.

Add the peppers, tomatoes, pinto beans, tomato paste and 200ml (7fl oz) water. Stir well to combine then add the thyme and bay leaf, season with salt and pepper and bring to a simmer.

Cook for 1–1½ hours over a low heat, uncovered, until the *guisado* reaches the consistency of a thick, rich stew, stirring occasionally and carefully with a wooden spoon so you do not mush the beans. Add more water if the *guisado* gets too dry. Remove from the heat, season to taste and serve with the following garnishes:

⚘ Ripe avocado cubed with salt and lemon juice
⚘ Pickled jalapeños (see page 273)
⚘ Habanero hot sauce (see page 284)
⚘ Coriander leaves
⚘ Snipped chives
⚘ Yoghurt or crème fraîche
⚘ Red pepper batons

Moors occupied Ibiza for some 400 years and the island retains many
of North Africa's warm spices, often the scent of a Can Riero winter.
The beef combined with orange peel and cinnamon is a great, unexpected
flavour combination. This *estofada* is perfect for entertaining as it is
best made a day ahead to allow the flavours to marry.

WINTER-SPICED CARNE ESTOFADA

Serves 8, with leftovers

✦ ✦ ✦ ✦ ✦ ✦ ✦ ✦ ✦ ✦ ✦

2kg (4lb 4oz) stewing
    beef chunks
45g (1¾oz) plain flour
1 tsp salt
1 tsp freshly ground black pepper
4 tbsp extra virgin olive oil
100g (3½oz) butter
120ml (4½fl oz) brandy
2 rosemary sprigs
1 stick celery, studded with
    6 whole cloves
6 sprigs thyme
Small handful flat-leaf
    parsley stems
Pared strips of peel from
    ½ orange
½ cinnamon stick
75g (3oz) bellota or Pata Negra
    ham offcuts (or Serrano
    ham or smoked pancetta)
3 onions, thinly sliced
5 garlic cloves, finely chopped
4 carrots, cut diagonally into 1cm
    (½in) thick slices
2 tbsp tomato paste
1½ bottles hearty Spanish
    red wine
750g (1lb 10oz) mixed
    mushrooms, cleaned and cut
    into even bite-sized pieces

Preheat the oven to 140°C (285°F), gas mark 2.

Pat the beef dry with kitchen paper (wet beef won't brown properly). Season the flour with the salt and pepper and divide the seasoned flour between 2 large resealable freezer bags. Divide the beef between the bags, then seal and shake until the meat is well coated in the flour.

Heat half the olive oil and half the butter in a large, heavy-based casserole dish over a medium-high heat. Brown the beef in batches, frying each batch for 5–6 minutes, tossing occasionally, until brown all over, then transfer to a bowl when done. Add more butter to the dish if needed.

When all the beef is browned, deglaze the dish with the brandy, scraping up any bits stuck to the bottom of the dish while it sizzles, and cook for 3–5 minutes to reduce the liquid by half, then pour it over the beef.

Tie the rosemary, celery, thyme, parsley stems, orange peel and cinnamon together with string, or wrap them all in a piece of muslin and tie the top shut.

Heat 25g (1oz) of the butter in a clean casserole dish, add the ham and fry for 2–3 minutes, then add the onions, garlic and carrots and fry for a further 7–9 minutes, until slightly golden. Add the tomato paste and cook for 1–2 minutes, then add the beef with its juices and the bundle of aromatics and pour in enough wine to nearly cover. Partially cover the casserole dish with a lid and bake in the oven for 3–4 hours, checking it periodically to ensure it is at a low simmer, reducing the heat if it is cooking too fast. The *estofada* is done when the liquid is rich and beef is very tender.

Heat the remaining oil and butter in a heavy-based frying pan, add the mushrooms and fry for 3–5 minutes, until slightly tender. Add them to the *estofada* just before the 3–4 hours cooking time is up, and stir to combine. Set the dish aside for at least 30 minutes (ideally overnight) before serving.

Moroccan food is popular on Ibiza. Some local restaurants have weekly couscous days. Our favourite is at Can Curune, which is always overflowing with north-of-the-island locals chatting and feasting. The warm, rich and fragrant taste of Morocco is a pleasure on a wet day.

MOROCCAN CHICKEN STEW

Serves 4

❦ ❦ ❦ ❦ ❦ ❦ ❦ ❦ ❦ ❦ ❦ ❦

2 tbsp extra virgin olive oil

1 large organic, free-range
   chicken (about 2kg/4lb 4oz),
   cut into 6 pieces

2 large onions, thinly sliced

2 sticks celery, thinly sliced

3 garlic cloves, finely chopped

1 fresh red chilli, deseeded
   and finely chopped

3cm (1¼in) piece root ginger,
   peeled and grated

1 tsp cumin seeds, toasted
   in a dry frying pan

2 tsp coriander seeds, toasted
   in a dry frying pan

1 cinnamon stick

1 pinch saffron threads

1 whole star anise

5 cloves, crushed

1 tsp pimentón dulce
   (sweet paprika)

150ml (5fl oz) white wine

500ml (18fl oz) chicken stock

4 plum tomatoes, peeled and
   roughly chopped

8 small waxy potatoes,
   peeled and cubed

3 carrots, cut diagonally into
   2.5cm (1in) thick slices

10 dried apricots

2 tsp harissa, to serve

Coriander leaves, to serve

Couscous (see page 254),
   to serve

Heat the olive oil in a large, heavy enamel or cast-iron casserole dish then fry the chicken pieces in batches, for 2–3 minutes on each side, until brown all over. Transfer the chicken pieces to a plate and set aside.

Add the onions and celery to the dish and cook for 6–7 minutes until softened, then add the garlic, chilli, ginger, chicken and spices to the pan, along with the wine. Bring to the boil and simmer for 2–3 minutes to reduce the wine slightly, then add the stock, together with the tomatoes, potatoes, carrots and apricots.

Reduce the heat, cover and simmer for 45 minutes, or alternatively place the dish in a 180°C (350°F), gas mark 4, oven for 45 minutes. Insert a meat thermometer into the thickest piece of chicken to check that the chicken is fully cooked – it should be 74°C (165°F). Once the chicken is cooked, set the oven grill to hot and cook the chicken under the grill for 2–3 minutes to crisp up the skin. Remove from the grill, discard the cinnamon stick and whole star anise and garnish with harissa and chopped coriander. I like to serve the stew with couscous.

The combination of dry brine and high-heat roasting produces
a moist, tender, flavourful, crisp-skinned bird that is fabulous served
with roasted vegetables and our *Samfaina* Jam (see page 280).

LEMON AND HERB ROAST CHICKEN WITH SAMFAINA JAM

Serves 4

❧ ❧ ❧ ❧ ❧ ❧ ❧ ❧ ❧ ❧ ❧

1 large organic free-range
    chicken
3 tbsp very coarse sea salt
    or kosher salt
1 lemon, poked all over
    with a skewer
5 rosemary sprigs
5 thyme sprigs
2–3 dried bay leaves, crushed
4 tbsp white wine
Salt and black pepper
250g (9oz) *Samfaina* Jam
    (see page 280), to serve

To dry brine: rub the chicken inside and out with the sea salt. Put it in a large plastic bag or wrap it tightly in clingfilm and put it in a bowl. Transfer to the fridge and chill for at least 2 hours (ideally overnight).

Preheat the oven to 220°C (430°F), gas mark 7. Remove the excess salt from the chicken skin and cavity, place the chicken in a roasting tin and stuff the cavity with the lemon, rosemary, thyme and crushed bay leaves and leave it for 30 minutes to come to room temperature.

Season the chicken lightly with pepper, roast for 20 minutes, then reduce the heat to 180°C (350°F), gas mark 4. Roast it for a further 20–30 minutes, depending on its size, or until a meat thermometer inserted into the thickest part of the chicken reads 74°C (165°F). Remove the chicken from the oven and transfer it to a serving dish to rest.

Pour off the fat and deglaze the roasting tin with the white wine, scraping the delicious brown bits up from the bottom of the tin. Bring it to the boil, let it bubble and reduce for 3–4 minutes, then strain through a sieve into a heatproof bowl. Drizzle the chicken with the pan juices and serve with *Samfaina* Jam.

❧ ❧ ❧

Tip: Save the leftover chicken carcass and meat for the Chicken and Bean soup (see page 238) and the Chicken Mushroom and Thyme Croquettes (see page 241).

Do not rinse the salt off from the dry brine. Knock off the excess against the sink or wipe it off with kitchen paper. Rinsing adds water to the bird, preventing the skin from crisping.

This is really a meal soup, richer, thicker and more like a stew. I use organic store-bought stock as a base and enrich it with the leftover chicken bones to make a double stock. Another option would be to collect the bones from several chickens and prepare a whole stock from there. As we eat a gorgeous chicken soup at least every other week, we can never seem to save up enough.

CHICKEN AND BEAN SOUP WITH CHORIZO AND KALE

Serves 6

Chicken carcass leftover from
   Lemon and Herb Roast Chicken
   (page 236), meat picked off
3 litres (5¼ pints) chicken stock
1 onion, studded with 10 cloves
1 carrot, cut into thin rounds
2 tbsp extra virgin olive oil
3 cooking chorizo (dulce or picante),
   skin removed and meat crumbled
6 onions, finely chopped
1 small head garlic, cloves
   finely chopped
3 red peppers, deseeded and
   finely chopped
2–3 tbsp pimentón dulce (sweet)
1½ tbsp pimentón picante (hot)
¼ tsp cayenne pepper
750g (1lb 10oz) Grated Tomatoes
   (see page 275)
500g (1lb 2oz) cooked white beans
   (see page 276)
1–1½ tbsp aged sherry vinegar
2 tsp agave syrup or caster sugar
2 fresh bay leaves
1 tsp dried thyme
1 large bunch kale, tough
   stems removed and leaves
   roughly chopped
Salt and black pepper

Break up the chicken carcass, once all the meat has been stripped from it, and place the carcass pieces in a large saucepan or stock pot. Add the chicken stock, clove-studded onion and carrot and place over the heat. Bring to a simmer, skim the fat from the top then continue simmering, uncovered, for 30 minutes. Strain the stock through a sieve into a heatproof jug or pan.

Heat the olive oil in a heavy-based saucepan over a medium-high heat. Add the chorizo, onions, garlic and peppers and fry for 5–6 minutes, until the chorizo is slightly browned and the vegetables have softened. Stir in the pimentón dulce and picante and the cayenne pepper and fry for a further 2–3 minutes, then add the grated tomatoes, white beans, chicken meat, homemade stock, vinegar, agave, bay leaves and thyme, and season with salt and pepper. Simmer over a low heat, uncovered, for 30 minutes then add the kale and simmer for a further 10–15 minutes until all the vegetables are tender. Season to taste and serve with toasted *pan payés*.

This recipe is based on one from my friend Amanda Burton, an outstanding cook and long-time resident of southern Spain. We make this Spanish classic with leftover roasted chicken. Adding thyme and mushroom makes it a wonderful winter tapa with a glass of wine. For terrific fast food, freeze uncooked croquettes on a baking tray then store them in a freezer bag until ready to use.

CHICKEN, MUSHROOM AND THYME CROQUETTES

Makes 24 croquettes

❧ ❧ ❧ ❧ ❧ ❧ ❧ ❧ ❧ ❧ ❧ ❧

70g (3oz) butter
170g (6oz) plain flour
240ml (8½fl oz) warm
 chicken stock
240ml (8½fl oz) warm whole milk
2 pinches ground or freshly
 grated nutmeg
2 tbsp extra virgin olive oil
170g (6oz) chestnut or portobello
 mushrooms, finely chopped
2 tbsp white wine
¼ small sweet onion,
 finely chopped
1 garlic clove, crushed
2 sprigs thyme, leaves
 finely chopped
100g (3½oz) leftover roast
 chicken, shredded
3 eggs, beaten
200g (7oz) panko breadcrumbs
 or regular breadcrumbs
1 litre (1¾ pints) light olive oil,
 for frying
Salt and black pepper
Lemon wedges, to serve

❧ ❧ ❧

Tip: Keep the oil around 170°C (340°F) – about 20°C less than normal frying temperature. At too high a heat the croquettes burst open and the delicious filling runs out.

Heat the butter in a medium, heavy-based saucepan for 4–5 minutes over a medium heat, until melted and frothing. Add 40g (1½oz) of the flour a little at a time, whisking to prevent lumps, and cook for 5 minutes. The roux should thicken but not colour.

Combine the warm stock and milk and slowly whisk into the roux. When all is incorporated, season with a pinch of nutmeg, salt and pepper. Cook for 10 minutes until thick – heavy ribbons should sit on the surface when you lift the whisk. Transfer to a bowl, cover the surface of the roux to stop a skin forming, cool, then chill. The roux will thicken as it cools.

Meanwhile, make the croquette mixture. Heat the oil in a heavy-based saucepan over a medium heat and fry the mushrooms for 6–8 minutes, until all the liquid has evaporated, then add the wine. Once the wine has evaporated, add the onion, garlic and thyme. Cook for 7–10 minutes until the onion has softened and any liquid has evaporated. Season with salt and pepper, remove from the heat, add the chicken and mix together. Combine the roux and chicken, taste and adjust the seasoning if necessary. Transfer to a bowl, cover the surface of the roux with clingfilm and chill until firm.

When ready to assemble the croquettes, mix the remaining flour, nutmeg, and a pinch each of salt and pepper in a bowl. Put the eggs and breadcrumbs on separate plates. Scoop out a tablespoonful of the chicken mixture and shape into a cylinder. Roll this in the flour, dip into the beaten egg, then roll in breadcrumbs to completely coat. Repeat with all the mixture.

Heat the oil in a deep, heavy-based saucepan and maintain the temperature at 170°C (340°F). Fry the croquettes in batches for 3–4 minutes until golden, then remove with a slotted spoon and transfer to the lined plate to drain. Serve with lemon wedges.

Remember the slow-roasted marinated leg of lamb (see page 64) with the tip to throw the bone in the freezer? Well, here is where you can use it. The bone adds a surprising amount of lamb flavour to the lentils, beautifully complementing the merguez.

LENTILS WITH LAMB BONE AND MERGUEZ SAUSAGE

Serves 6

✦ ✦ ✦ ✦ ✦ ✦ ✦ ✦ ✦ ✦ ✦

5 tbsp extra virgin olive oil
2 onions, finely chopped
100g (3½oz) Grated Tomatoes
   (see page 275)
4 garlic cloves, finely chopped
3 leeks, trimmed, rinsed and
   sliced into 1cm (½in)
   thick rounds
4 carrots, finely chopped
3 dried bay leaves
340g (12oz) dried Pardina or
   puy lentils, rinsed thoroughly
½ tsp ground cumin
2 pinches cayenne pepper
750ml (25fl oz) vegetable stock
Bone from Slow-Roasted
   Marinated Leg of Lamb
   (see page 64)
Small handful thyme leaves
4 wide pared strips of peel
   from 1 lemon
3 tbsp aged sherry vinegar,
   plus 1 tsp for the lentils
350g (12oz) merguez sausages
Salt and black pepper

Heat 3 tablespoons of the olive oil in a large, heavy-based saucepan over a medium-high heat. Add the onions and grated tomatoes and fry for 8–10 minutes until the onions have softened, then add the garlic, leeks, carrots and bay leaves and fry for a further 5 minutes.

Tip in the rinsed lentils, then add the cumin and cayenne. Fry for 5 minutes then add the stock, lamb bone, thyme and strips of lemon peel. Bring to a simmer and cook uncovered for 20–25 minutes. Add 1 teaspoon of the sherry vinegar, season with salt and pepper, then cook for a further 5–10 minutes, until the lentils are *al dente* and most of the liquid has been absorbed.

Meanwhile, heat the remaining olive oil in a heavy-based frying pan and line a plate with kitchen paper. Add the merguez to the hot pan and fry for 6–8 minutes, turning them frequently, until brown all over, then transfer to the lined plate. Deglaze the sausage pan with the aged sherry vinegar, then add the browned merguez sausages and pan liquid to the lentils and serve immediately.

Burgers made with local lamb are a winter staple at Can Riero. A great comfort food, particularly on a cold, wet night, they are best enjoyed curled up on the sofa with dinner trays in front of the fire. Serving Patatas Bravas (see page 293) on the side makes this an entirely decadent meal. Serve with extra bravas sauce and creamy Dijon mustard, too.

IBERIAN LAMB BURGER WITH CARAMELISED ONIONS AND YOGHURT SAUCE

Serves 4

❦ ❦ ❦ ❦ ❦ ❦ ❦ ❦ ❦ ❦ ❦

800g (1¾lb) lamb mince (ask your butcher to grind a mix of neck and leg meat, or buy pre-packaged good-quality mince)
Extra virgin olive oil, for brushing and greasing
4 hamburger buns, halved, to serve
250g (9oz) Caramelised Onions (see page 273)
100g (3½oz) Cucumber and Onion Pickles (see page 277)
80g (3¼oz) feta cheese, crumbled
1 large ripe tomato, sliced
4 fresh lettuce leaves
60g (2½oz) pitted black olives
Patatas Bravas (see page 293)
Salt and black pepper

Yoghurt sauce
¼ onion, finely chopped
50g (2oz) full-fat yoghurt
50g (2oz) crème fraîche
½ tsp grated lemon zest
2 garlic cloves, crushed
1 tsp capers, finely chopped

Shape the lamb mince into 4 patties, being careful not to overwork the meat, as this will toughen it. Lightly oil the patties, season with salt and pepper and set aside on a plate.

Assemble all the ingredients for the yoghurt sauce in a small bowl, mix well, and season to taste. Heat a barbecue grill or griddle pan to hot.

Brush the cut surfaces of the buns with olive oil, then toast them cut side down for 2 minutes on the grill to give them nice grill marks. Set aside.

Cook the lamb burgers on the hot grill or griddle pan for 3–4 minutes on each side. Do not move them while they are cooking.

To assemble, spread the yoghurt sauce on the bottom halves of the toasted buns. Place the burgers on top, and top with equal portions of caramelised onions, pickles, crumbled feta, tomato slices, lettuce and olives, top with the other half of the bun and serve immediately with patatas bravas.

❦ ❦ ❦

Tip: The neck meat is much less expensive but very flavourful. Mixing it with ground leg or shoulder meat makes this a perfect burger.

This stew is elegant and rich, great for a festive occasion. Its truly special flavour starts with the Catalan *picada*, a base made with fried bread, nuts, garlic, herbs and oil.

LOBSTER, PRAWN AND SCALLOP STEW

Serves 6

❧ ❧ ❧ ❧ ❧ ❧ ❧ ❧ ❧ ❧ ❧ ❧

4 tbsp extra virgin olive oil
500g (1lb 2oz) large whole
　raw Mediterranean or
　Atlantic prawns, peeled
　and digestive tracts
　removed, shells reserved
500g (1lb 2oz) clams,
　cleaned and scrubbed
½ onion, thinly sliced
2 cooked lobsters (about
　1.5kg/3lb 4oz in total),
　meat picked, shells reserved
Large handful flat-leaf
　parsley
2 garlic cloves, finely chopped
40g (1½oz) toasted blanched
　almonds, chopped
2 Roasted Tomatoes
　(see page 275)
1 slice fried bread, crumbled
½ tsp salt
1 tbsp plain white flour
125ml (4½fl oz) white wine
1.5 litres (2½ pints) stock
300g (11oz) shucked scallops
Black pepper

To make the stock base, heat 1 tablespoon of the olive oil in a heavy-based frying pan and fry the prawn shells for 3–5 minutes until they are dry, then add another tablespoon of olive oil, the onion and lobster shells and fry for 2–3 minutes. Put the fried shells and onion in a large saucepan with 2 litres of water and the parsley, retaining some parsley to garnish. Bring to the boil then reduce the heat and simmer, uncovered, for 30 minutes. Strain and set aside.

Meanwhile, crush the garlic and almonds in a mortar and pestle to make a thick paste. Place the roasted tomatoes, crumbled fried bread, garlic and almond paste in the bowl of a food processor or blender with the salt and blitz until smooth. Add a splash of white wine if you want a smooth texture.

Heat the remaining oil, add the tomato and bread mixture, then pour in the stock and the white wine. Stir well to get rid of any lumps, bring to a simmer and cook over a low heat, uncovered, for 15 minutes.

Add the scallops to the stew and poach them for 2–3 minutes until just cooked – they should be somewhat firm but still springy to the touch. Remove the scallops with a slotted spoon and set aside. Add the prawns and poach for 1–1½ minutes until just opaque. Remove and set aside with the scallops. Add the clams and cook for 2–3 minutes or until the shells are open. Remove, discarding any clams that have not opened, and set aside with the rest of the shellfish.

Divide the scallops, prawns, clams and lobster meat evenly among six bowls, then ladle the hot stock into the bowls, sprinkle each with flat-leaf parsley and black pepper and serve.

❧ ❧ ❧

Tip: The key to this dish is to not overcook the seafood – flavour and texture are equally important. Overdone prawns and lobster become chewy and difficult to cut; scallops become rubbery. Not an elegant result. To avoid this, cook one type of seafood at a time. Remove each to a plate just as it goes opaque, so it will cool quickly and halt the cooking process. Ask your fishmonger to part-cook the lobsters so they can be finished in the hot broth.

The magnificence of this pasta lies in its utter simplicity and great ingredients. It literally takes as long to make as the pasta does to boil. Use finest-quality clams, and get lots. We use handmade black squid ink spaghetti from Matteo, the Italian proprietor of the Il Pirata del Tortello pasta shop on Formentera.

CLAMS WITH SQUID INK PASTA, CHILLI AND GARLIC

Serves 4

✿ ✿ ✿ ✿ ✿ ✿ ✿ ✿ ✿ ✿

500g (1lb 2oz) squid ink pasta
4 tbsp extra virgin olive oil,
    plus extra for drizzling
5 garlic cloves, finely chopped
1 fresh or dried red chilli,
    deseeded and finely chopped
2kg (4lb 4oz) fresh
    medium clams, rinsed and
    thoroughly scrubbed
225–350ml (8–12fl oz)
    white wine
Handful coriander,
    leaves chopped
Salt and black pepper

Cook the pasta according to the packet instructions, and drain.

Heat half the olive oil in a large, heavy-based frying pan (with a lid) over a medium-high heat. Add the garlic and chilli and fry for 5–6 minutes, until softened and golden, then add the clams and toss to coat. Pour in enough white wine to cover the bottom of the pan to 0.5cm (¼in) deep. Cover and bring to the boil. Cook for 8–10 minutes, shaking occasionally – check after 8 minutes, and when most of the clams are open remove the lid to reduce the liquid, tossing the clams occasionally to keep them moist. Remove the pan from the heat, discarding any clams that remain closed, add the coriander and toss to combine.

Toss the cooked pasta with the remaining olive oil and season with salt and pepper. Pour the clams over the top of the pasta and drizzle with olive oil to serve.

✿ ✿ ✿

Tip: If fresh squid ink pasta is unavailable, use a good-quality dried squid ink spaghetti instead.

The base of this dish uses the classic *sofregit* – onions slow-cooked in olive oil with tomatoes and infused with herbs. Traditionally, *sofregit* is made with onions and tomatoes but it can incorporate other vegetables, most often garlic and red and green peppers. Cook it very slowly to intensify the flavours of the vegetables. It is a great foundation for this delicious vegetarian shared plate.

WHITE BEANS WITH FENNEL AND POLENTA IN ROASTED TOMATO SAUCE

Serves 6

500g (1lb 2oz) instant polenta
2 tbsp extra virgin olive oil, plus extra for brushing
5 onions, 3 thinly sliced and 2 thickly sliced
500g (1lb 2oz) Grated Tomatoes (about 6 tomatoes – see page 275)
4 garlic cloves, finely chopped
Splash sherry
2 sprigs rosemary, leaves finely chopped
Small handful thyme, leaves finely chopped
600g (1¼lb) cooked white haricot beans, drained, or 2 x 400g (14oz) tins of haricot beans, drained and rinsed
120–240ml (4½–8½fl oz) vegetable stock
2 fennel bulbs, thickly sliced (fronds reserved for garnish)
6 Roasted Tomatoes (see page 275), halved
200g (7oz) Roasted Tomato Sauce (see page 282)
40g (1½oz) aged Mahón or Pecorino cheese, grated (optional)
Salt and black pepper

Cook the polenta according to the packet instructions, transfer to a 23cm (9in) square baking tin and leave to cool.

Meanwhile, heat the olive oil in a large, heavy-based saucepan over a medium-high heat, add the 3 thinly sliced onions and fry for 5 minutes, then reduce the heat to low and continue to cook the onions for 15–20 minutes, until soft and slightly golden. Do not brown.

Add the grated tomatoes, garlic and sherry and season with salt and pepper. Cook for 8–10 minutes, until the vegetables are soft and amalgamated, then stir in the rosemary and thyme and cook for a further 2 minutes. Add the white beans and gently stir them through the mixture, taking care not to crush them, then add just enough stock to cover the bottom of the pan. Cover and simmer over a low heat for 20 minutes.

While the beans are cooking, brush the thickly sliced onion and fennel on both sides with olive oil and grill under a hot grill, or on a griddle pan or barbecue, for 10–15 minutes, until *al dente* and slightly browned. Remove the white beans from the heat and season to taste.

Cut the cooled polenta into 6 pieces, brush with oil on both sides, sprinkle with salt and place on a baking sheet. Grill under a hot grill, or on a griddle pan or barbecue, for 1–2 minutes on each side until crisp and hot through.

Layer the grilled polenta, roasted tomatoes, onion, fennel and white beans on individual plates.

Top with roasted tomato sauce, and serve sprinkled with grated cheese and fennel fronds, if you like.

The Catalan combination of spinach and chickpeas is delicious topped with a drizzle of olive oil and served as a side dish, but adding pumpkin, lemon couscous and walnut sage *picada* transforms it into a warming meal. It is equally good served with spelt, orzo or quinoa.

SPINACH, CHICKPEAS AND BUTTERNUT SQUASH WITH COUSCOUS AND WALNUT AND SAGE PICADA

Serves 4

❦ ❦ ❦ ❦ ❦ ❦ ❦ ❦ ❦ ❦ ❦

1 medium butternut squash, deseeded, peeled and cut into 12 x 3cm (1¼in) thick slices
3 tbsp extra virgin olive oil, plus 4 tbsp olive oil, for brushing
1kg (2lb 2oz) fresh spinach leaves, rinsed
250g (9oz) extra-large cooked chickpeas (see page 276), drained and patted dry with kitchen paper
4 small garlic cloves, thinly sliced
1 small onion, thinly sliced
Splash white wine
Salt and black pepper
Handful toasted pine nuts, to serve

To make the picada, put the walnuts in a heatproof bowl, cover with boiling water and leave to soak for 30 minutes, then drain, tip onto a clean tea towel and rub gently to remove the skins. Put the walnuts and sage in the bowl of a food processor and pulse until the walnuts are finely chopped. Add the remaining ingredients and pulse until the sauce is nearly smooth. Season with salt and pepper and pulse again to combine. Transfer to a bowl and set aside.

To cook the couscous, mix the olive oil, lemon juice and water in a bowl. Stir the couscous into the liquid along with salt, pepper and cayenne, cover with a plate and let sit for 30 minutes. Preheat the oven to 200°C (400°F), gas mark 6.

Brush or rub the squash slices all over with olive oil, sprinkle with salt and pepper and roast on a baking tray for 20–25 minutes, until nearly tender, then turn on the grill to medium and grill the roasted squash for 2–3 minutes on each side until golden. Remove from the grill and turn the oven on again, to 180°C (350°F), gas mark 4.

When the couscous has absorbed the water, remove the plate and rake through with a fork to separate the grains. Spread the couscous out on a baking sheet and bake for 15–20 minutes until light and fluffy, then remove from the oven and transfer to a serving dish, stir through the lemon zest, fluff up with a fork and season with salt and pepper.

Lemon couscous
1 tbsp extra virgin olive oil
Juice of 1 lemon
220ml (8fl oz) water,
   at room temperature
165g (5¾oz) couscous
Pinch cayenne pepper
Grated zest of ½ lemon
Salt and black pepper

Walnut, sage and chilli picada
100g (3½oz) walnuts
3–4 sage leaves, veins removed
   and leaves chopped
¼ fresh bird's eye chilli,
   deseeded and finely chopped
2–3 tsp single cream
2–3 tbsp extra virgin olive oil
Salt and black pepper

Heat 1 tablespoon of the olive oil in a large frying pan over a high heat. When it is very hot, add a handful of the spinach, with a couple of pinches of salt. Toss with tongs to wilt evenly, then remove and place in a colander. Repeat with the remaining spinach, wilting it a handful at a time, and set aside.

Add another tablespoon of olive oil to the pan, reheat until hot, then add the drained and dried chickpeas. Cook for 4–5 minutes, shaking the pan so they brown but don't burn. Transfer the chickpeas to the colander with the spinach.

Add another tablespoon of olive oil to the pan, reheat until hot, then fry the garlic and onion over a medium heat for 10–12 minutes, until soft and lightly browned. Add a splash of white wine and stir until nearly evaporated – the texture should be jam-like. Add the spinach and chickpeas, toss and cook for 2–3 minutes to warm through. Remove from the heat.

To serve, layer the couscous, spinach and roasted squash on a serving dish. Drizzle with walnut, sage and chilli piacada and the pine nuts.

⋆ ⋆ ⋆

Tip: The recipe here makes perfect, fluffy couscous. Steeping it in room-temperature water allows the couscous to absorb the water without overcooking. The lemon juice and salt add huge flavour, while the oven removes any extra moisture.

Flaó is a classic Ibicencan tart traditionally made with a caraway-studded pastry crust and filled with fresh goat's cheese (*queso fresco*) and wild spearmint. Although closely associated with Easter, it is eaten all year round. Our adaption combines creamy mascarpone with ricotta and incorporates mint into a sauce made with the home-grown strawberries which we freeze each spring.

FLAÓ WITH STRAWBERRY MINT SAUCE

Serves 8–10

❦ ❦ ❦ ❦ ❦ ❦ ❦ ❦ ❦ ❦ ❦

You will need: 23cm (9in) round, fluted, loose-bottomed tart tin

300g (11oz) plain flour, plus extra for dusting
3 tbsp caster sugar
½ tsp salt
180g (6oz) unsalted butter
2–3 tbsp milk
4 tbsp vodka

Filling
3 eggs
125g (4½oz) caster sugar
250g (9oz) mascarpone
250g (9oz) ricotta
Grated zest of 1 lemon
2–3 tbsp lemon juice
1 tsp fine salt

Strawberry and mint sauce
250g (9oz) strawberries, fresh or frozen, hulled
3–5 tbsp caster sugar
2 tsp lemon juice
½ tsp freshly ground black pepper
Large handful mint leaves, cut into ribbons

To make the pastry, combine the flour, sugar and salt in a bowl. Add the butter, milk and vodka and combine to form a ball. Wrap the dough in clingfilm and chill for 15 minutes. Preheat the oven to 160°C (320°F), gas mark 3.

Roll out the chilled dough on a floured non-stick work surface until it is 3mm thick, then use it to line the tart tin. Put the pastry-lined tin back in the fridge to chill for 30 minutes, then line the pastry with baking paper and fill it with baking beans, dried beans or uncooked rice. Bake for 10–12 minutes, then remove the beans and paper and bake for a further 5 minutes, until the crust is dry to the touch but not brown. Remove from the oven and set aside (leaving the oven on).

To make the filling, beat the eggs and sugar together in the bowl of a stand mixer or with a hand-held mixer until pale and fluffy and the whisk leaves thick ribbons in the mixture when you lift it. Add the mascarpone and ricotta, beat to incorporate then stir in the lemon zest and juice and salt. Pour the mixture into the blind-baked pastry tart case and bake for 30–40 minutes, until the edges are set and the centre is slightly wobbly. Remove from the oven and leave to cool before turning the tart out of the tin.

To make the strawberry and mint sauce, place the strawberries, 3 tablespoons of the sugar and all the lemon juice in a bowl or jug and purée with a hand-held blender (alternatively, blitz in the bowl of a food processor). Taste and add more sugar if necessary, to achieve the desired sweetness. Stir in the pepper and mint ribbons and drizzle the sauce over the cooled *flaó*. Serve immediately.

Delightfully retro, individual baked Alaskas make an impressive finish. The multiple layers of hazelnut flavour from the ice cream, Frangelico and chopped nuts make it an intense, sweet, yet sophisticated dessert.

BAKED ALASKA WITH ITALIAN MERINGUE

Serves 6

❧ ❧ ❧ ❧ ❧ ❧ ❧ ❧ ❧ ❧ ❧

You will need: a piping bag fitted with a round nozzle and a blowtorch

Frangelico soaking syrup
30g caster sugar
4 tbsp water
1½ tbsp Frangelico or other hazelnut liqueur

1 *Pastel de Mantequilla* cake (see page 285)
500g (1lb 2oz) hazelnut ice cream
1 x quantity Italian Meringue (see page 286)
3 tbsp toasted hazelnuts, roughly chopped

Line a baking tray with baking paper.

To make the syrup, place the sugar and water in a small saucepan and bring to a rolling boil, stirring constantly. Add the liqueur. Stir to combine and set aside. When cool, transfer to a small jar with a lid. The syrup can be made up to 2 days in advance.

Cut the *Pastel de Mantequilla* into 6 rounds using a round 6cm (2½in) cutter, and place the rounds on the baking tray. Using a toothpick, poke holes halfway through the depth of the cake, all over the rounds. Using a pastry or basting brush, baste the rounds liberally with the Frangelico soaking syrup.

Place a scoop of hazelnut ice cream on top of each sponge round and quickly pipe the meringue around the sponge and ice cream in a circular motion, starting at the base and coming to a peak at the top. Use the flat edge of a knife to smooth out the meringue, leaving small peaks.

Working quickly, repeat with the other sponges. Transfer the tray to the freezer for 30 minutes, to set, then remove and brown the meringue using a blowtorch. Garnish with hazelnuts and serve immediately.

❧ ❧ ❧

Tip: Prepare the dessert in advance by making the cake ahead, topping with ice cream and meringue and freezing. Pull it out and brown the meringue just before serving.

This compote is a delicious use of Can Riero's sun-dried figs, though shop-bought dried figs work nearly as well. With its wine and spice, Christmas holidays come to mind. We like to spoon it over yoghurt for a festive brunch.

WINTER-SPICED DRIED FRUIT COMPOTE

Serves 4

375ml (13fl oz) fruity
   young red wine
3 tbsp caster sugar, or to taste
1 cinnamon stick
120g (4½oz) dried cherries
150g (5oz) dried apricots
180g (6oz) dried figs
Grated zest of ½ orange
Juice from ¼ orange

Combine the wine, sugar and cinnamon stick in a small saucepan and bring it to the boil over a medium-high heat. Reduce the heat and let the wine simmer slowly for 15–20 minutes, to boil off the alcohol, steep the cinnamon and allow the sugar to dissolve.

Add the fruit and orange zest and increase the heat to medium-high to return it to a simmer, then reduce the heat again and gently simmer the fruit for about 20 minutes, until it is plump and tender, tasting after 10 minutes to check the sweetness. Add more sugar if desired. The compote is done when the fruit is plump and rehydrated, but not mushy.

Squeeze in the orange juice to brighten the flavour then let the fruit cool in the pan, allowing the fruit and wine flavours to marry. Serve at just above room temperature with lemon biscuits (see page 264), or as a topping for ice cream.

Tip: Start by adding 3 tablespoons of sugar and taste as you cook. Every wine will require a different degree of added sweetness, so you may want to add more.

This buttery, citrusy shortbread biscuit with candied lemon slices tastes as good as it is beautiful. It pairs especially well with the wine and fruit compote on page 262, but is equally delightful with strong black coffee (*café solo*) or a granita (see page 134).

LEMON BISCUITS

Makes 18 biscuits

❦ ❦ ❦ ❦ ❦ ❦ ❦ ❦ ❦ ❦ ❦

180g (6oz) plain flour,
    plus extra for dusting
60g (2½oz) caster sugar,
    plus extra for sprinkling
125g (4½oz) unsalted butter,
    chilled and diced
Grated zest of 1 lemon
1 tbsp lemon juice

Candied lemon
150ml (5fl oz) water
150g (5oz) caster sugar
2 large lemons, sliced into
    ½cm (¼in) thick rounds

To make the candied lemon, line a plate with non-stick baking paper and bring the water to the boil in a large frying pan over a medium-high heat. Add the sugar to the boiling water and stir until it completely dissolves. Cover the bottom of the pan with a single layer of lemon slices, reduce the heat and simmer for 6–8 minutes, until the lemon becomes translucent. Transfer the fruit to the lined plate and repeat the cooking process with the remaining slices. Set aside until ready to serve.

To make the biscuit dough, combine the flour and sugar in a bowl then rub the cold butter into the flour and sugar with your fingertips until the mixture resembles breadcrumbs. Add the lemon zest and juice, combine, then form the dough into a ball, wrap it in clingfilm and transfer the dough to the fridge to chill for 30 minutes –1 hour. Preheat the oven to 180°C (350°F), gas mark 4.

Roll out the chilled dough on a floured non-stick work surface to a thickness of 0.5cm (¼in). Sprinkle it with sugar then cut out about 18 rounds using a round 8cm (3in) cutter. Divide the rounds between 2 ungreased baking trays and bake for 15–20 minutes until the edges are just golden. Remove from the oven, transfer the biscuits to a wire rack and allow to cool. Top with a slice of candied lemon to serve.

Kumquat is an astonishing citrus fruit. The rind is sweet and the flesh tart, nearly as acidic as lemon. Here it gives the freshness of lemon with a unique perfume-like flavour. Paired with pistachio and polenta, it is delicious.

POLENTA, PISTACHIO AND KUMQUAT CAKE

Serves 8–10

❦ ❦ ❦ ❦ ❦ ❦ ❦ ❦ ❦ ❦ ❦

You will need: 24cm (9½in) round springform cake tin

250g (9oz) unsalted butter, softened, plus extra for greasing
200g (7oz) caster sugar
Grated zest of 1 orange
3 eggs, at room temperature
3 tbsp pistachio paste
80ml (3¼fl oz) freshly squeezed kumquat juice (you will need about 150g fresh kumquats)
125g (4½oz) instant polenta, plus extra for sprinkling
225g (8oz) ground pistachios, plus extra chopped pistachios to decorate (optional)
½ tsp fine salt
1½ tsp baking powder

Glaze
2 tbsp kumquat juice
100g (3½oz) icing sugar

Preheat the oven to 180°C (350°F), gas mark 4, grease the cake tin and sprinkle it with polenta. Line the base of the tin with baking paper and set aside.

Cream together the butter, sugar and orange zest in the bowl of a stand mixer fitted with the paddle attachment, or in a bowl with an electric hand-held mixer, until light and fluffy. Add the eggs one at a time, beating well after each addition, then beat in the pistachio paste and kumquat juice.

Combine the polenta, ground pistachios, salt and baking powder in a separate bowl. Add the dry ingredients to the butter, sugar and egg mixture in 3 equal portions, gently but thoroughly incorporating each addition before adding the next. Pour the batter into the prepared tin and bake for 40–45 minutes, or until a skewer inserted into the centre of the cake comes out clean.

Meanwhile, whisk all the glaze ingredients together until smooth and glossy, then set aside.

Remove the cake from the oven, let it cool a little, then run a sharp knife around the inside of the pan, open the tin's catch and remove the cake. Remove the base of the tin from the cake, set the cake on a wire rack and allow to cool completely. Drizzle the glaze over the cake once it is completely cool and scatter with chopped pistachios, if you like.

Panellets are a Catalan delicacy that usually make an appearance on the 1st of November, *Día de Todos los Santos* (All Saints Day), and are enjoyed throughout the holiday season and winter. They are the perfect grown-up festive nibble: rich, elegant in flavour, sumptuous in texture. They pair beautifully with dessert wine, too.

PANALLETS
(PINE NUT COOKIES)
Makes 28 cookies

✢ ✢ ✢ ✢ ✢ ✢ ✢ ✢ ✢ ✢ ✢

1 medium sweet potato, peeled
    and cut into 1cm (½in) cubes
275g (10oz) caster sugar
2 eggs, separated
1½ tsp Grand Marnier
    or vanilla extract
375g (13oz) ground almonds
Finely grated zest of 1 orange
350g (12oz) pine nuts
Salt

Preheat the oven to 170°C (340°F), gas mark 4, and line 2 baking trays with baking paper.

Put the sweet potato in a saucepan, cover with water, add a pinch of salt and bring to the boil. Reduce the heat and simmer over a medium heat for 10–12 minutes until tender. Drain, transfer to a bowl, mash well and leave to cool.

Add the sugar to the cooled sweet potato and stir to combine. The mixture will liquefy slightly.

Lightly beat the egg yolks with the Grand Marnier or vanilla. Add the yolks to the sweet potato mixture with the almonds and orange zest. Stir thoroughly to form a stiff paste that has the consistency of marzipan. Roll a heaped tablespoon of the dough (about 30g/1¼oz) into a ball and set aside on a plate. Repeat until all the dough is used up and you have about 28 balls.

Lightly beat the egg whites with a teaspoon of water to make an egg wash, and distribute the pine nuts on a plate in an even layer. Dip a ball of the cookie dough in the egg wash, shake off the excess, and roll it in the pine nuts. Press the nuts into the ball gently but firmly to evenly cover the surface. Fill in any gaps with extra nuts. Place on the baking tray and repeat with the remaining balls. Bake for 20–25 minutes, until golden, checking them regularly as pine nuts burn easily (remove the biscuits from the oven if they start to singe). Remove from the oven and leave to cool on the trays. The biscuits will keep well in an airtight tin in a cool, dry place for up to 4 days.

✢ ✢ ✢

Tip: Toast any leftover pine nuts on the plate for 3–4 minutes until brown, and eat immediately or store separately as they will have traces of egg on them, and so need to be sufficiently heated and stored separately.

BASICS AND ACCOMPANIMENTS

BASIC RECIPES

CARAMELISED ONIONS

Makes about 675g (24 oz)

Caramelised onions are the most delicious and versatile of onion preparations. Slightly creamy, sweet and rich, they form a cornerstone of our cooking at Can Riero. Use them as a base for soups and stews, or as an essential topping for the Iberian Lamb Burger (see page 245). They are a delicious addition to sandwiches, egg dishes and charcuterie plates, too.

❦ ❦ ❦ ❦ ❦ ❦ ❦ ❦ ❦ ❦ ❦

4 tbsp light olive oil
1.5kg (3lb 4oz) onions, thinly sliced
¼ tsp brown sugar (optional)
½ tsp sherry vinegar (optional)
Salt and black pepper

Heat half the oil in a large, heavy-based frying pan over a medium-high heat, then add the onions, 2 pinches of salt and a couple of turns of the pepper mill. Reduce the heat to low and stir the onions into the olive oil. The oil will quickly be absorbed. If the pan is too dry, add another tablespoon of oil and stir to combine. Fry slowly over a very low heat for 20 minutes, until the onions are soft and beginning to break down. Taste, and if they are not sweet and flavourful enough, add the brown sugar, ¼ teaspoon salt and a pinch of ground black pepper. Continue to cook over a low heat for 30–40 minutes, uncovered, until the onions reach a jam-like consistency. Remove from the heat and adjust seasoning to taste, adding the vinegar, if desired, to lift the flavour.

❦ ❦ ❦

Tip: The vinegar will soften the onions further, so only add it at the end of the cooking time if eating immediately. If storing the onions for another time, add the vinegar just before serving.

PICKLED JALAPEÑOS

Makes 450g (1lb)

These are delicious and terrific to have on hand. We began making them because jalepeños don't dry or keep well, we had a big yield and needed something to do with them. I make a big batch once a year so we have them to enjoy with sandwiches, sauces and, of course, Beef and Bean Guisado (see page 230).

❦ ❦ ❦ ❦ ❦ ❦ ❦ ❦ ❦ ❦ ❦

You will need: 500g (1lb 2oz) sterilised preserving jar with lid (see page 295)

450g (1lb) fresh jalapeño chillies, cut into 1cm (½in) thick slices
1 tbsp coarse salt, plus extra for salting
240ml (8½fl oz) white wine vinegar
2 tbsp caster sugar
4 tbsp water

Place the sliced jalapeños in a bowl, salt them lightly and set aside at room temperature for 1 hour.

Combine the vinegar, salt, sugar and water in a large saucepan and bring to the boil.

Rinse the jalapeños in a colander under cold running water to remove excess salt, shake off the excess water then leave to drain on kitchen paper or clean tea towels. Add them to the boiling liquid, return to the boil then immediately remove from the heat. Pour the pickled jalapeños into the sterilised jar and seal.

ROASTED RED PEPPERS

Makes 6

Roasted red peppers are a cornerstone of Catalan cuisine, where they are eaten on their own in olive oil, with roasted aubergine, or as a base for soups and sauces. Roasting completely transforms peppers, making them velvety soft, rich and sweet. Save the liquor from the roasting process and add it to a sauce.

There are two methods for roasting: using a gas hob, which produces velvety-textured peppers and a little more liquor, but can be a bit messy, and oven roasting, which is perfect for those who prefer less mess or don't have a gas hob. The trick is to completely char the surface of the pepper. The more charred it is, the better: that's how the pepper develops its sweet, smoky flavour. Its thick skin prevents the flesh from tasting like charcoal. If you've not charred peppers on the hob before, char them one at a time, so you have time to master the technique of managing the tongs while charring the entire surface of the pepper.

✿ ✿ ✿ ✿ ✿ ✿ ✿ ✿ ✿ ✿ ✿

6 large red peppers (about 1kg/2lb 2oz)

Method One:
Remove the grill from the hob, and turn all the burners except the smallest on high. Wash and dry the whole peppers, and place as many peppers as will comfortably fit directly onto the hob, using all of the burners. Grill them for 3–4 minutes on each side, turning them gently with long-handled tongs (ideally tongs with silicone tips, to avoid tearing the flesh) until charred and black all over. To grill the bottoms, lay a pepper on its side directing the bottom into the flame and hold the pepper with the tongs directly on the heat source to char any remaining skin. Transfer the charred peppers to a metal bowl and cover the bowl with a saucepan lid, until they are all done. Replace the lid after adding each charred pepper. The peppers will continue to cook as they cool, developing a rich, deep, smoky flavour. When

completely cool, strain any liquor that has accumulated in the bottom of the bowl into a clean bowl. Scrape and wipe the peppers to remove the charred skin. When they are clean, remove the stem, cut the peppers into quarters, remove the seeds and place the pepper quarters in the bowl with the liquor. Rinse the ash off your hands if necessary but do not wash the peppers, as this will dilute their flavour.

Method Two:
This two-step oven method involves oven roasting to cook, then grilling to char the skin.

Preheat the oven to 140°C (275°F), gas mark 1. Wash and dry the whole peppers. Place the peppers on a baking tray and bake them in the oven for 45 minutes. Remove from the oven, cut out and discard the stem, cut each pepper in half and remove the seeds. Flatten the halves with your hands, rub them with olive oil, then place on a baking sheet skin-side up. Place under a hot grill for 5 minutes until the skin is blackened and charred. Transfer to a metal bowl and cover the bowl with a saucepan lid. Peel as in Method One.

ROASTED TOMATOES
Makes 1kg (2lb 2oz)

Roasting tomatoes is a wonderful way to concentrate and enhance their flavour. They are a Can Riero staple, and their intensity adds a wonderful depth to sauces. It's worth making a big batch, even if a recipe calls for less, as they keep well. Pack the roasted tomatoes into sterilised glass jars, cover them in olive oil and chill for up to 2 weeks, or open-freeze on a baking tray then store in re-sealable freezer bags. They are lovely to have on hand. The longer and slower the tomatoes cook, the richer they will taste.

✤ ✤ ✤ ✤ ✤ ✤ ✤ ✤ ✤ ✤ ✤

2kg (4lb 4oz) tomatoes
Extra virgin olive oil
Salt and black pepper

Preheat the oven to 120°C (250°F), gas mark ½, lightly grease 2 baking trays with oil, and sprinkle the trays with salt and pepper. Halve the tomatoes lengthways and scoop out the seeds, either by squeezing the tomatoes over a bowl or using a spoon. Place the halved tomatoes on the trays, cut side down, and roast in the oven for 4 hours, or at 120°C (250°F), gas mark ½, for 3 hours, rotating the trays every hour to ensure the tomatoes are evenly cooked. The tomatoes are done when they are deep red, wrinkled, reduced in size by about half and the skins have curled away from the flesh and can be easily pinched off. Remove the trays from the oven and leave to one side until the tomatoes are cool enough to touch, then remove and discard the skins.

✤ ✤ ✤

Tip: Deglaze the trays with water or white wine. Put each tray over a medium-hot burner on the hob. When the pan is hot add 120ml (4½fl oz) of water or white wine. Use a spatula to scrape up the lovely browned bits. They are flavour bombs, well worth retrieving from the pan. Reduce the liquid by half or more. Pour it over the tomato halves or reserve to add to a recipe.

GRATED TOMATOES
Makes 600g (1¼ lb)

Grated tomatoes are an Ibicenco staple used to make *Pan con Tomate* (see page 285), moisten *bocadillos* and form the base of many sauces, stews and soups. Although there is a special tomato for this staple, the *tomate de colgar*, most salad tomatoes will do nicely.

✤ ✤ ✤ ✤ ✤ ✤ ✤ ✤ ✤ ✤ ✤

1kg (2lb 2 oz) salad tomatoes

Halve the tomatoes across their middle (not lengthways). Remove the seeds and juice by gently squeezing the tomatoes over a bowl. Use a spoon to scrape out any remaining seeds. Strain the seeds from the juice using a fine-mesh sieve and discard the seeds. Hold the skin side of each tomato over the bowl of juice and shred the tomato flesh against the large holes of a box grater. Gradually and gently grate the tomatoes until just the skin remains. Discard the skins. When all of the tomatoes are grated, mix the juice and flesh together and the grated tomatoes are ready to use.

COOKING PULSES

Pulses such as beans and chickpeas cooked at home have a firmer texture and don't break up as easily as tinned pulses, and are less expensive, too. Cook them in 1kg (2lb 2oz) batches and freeze the extra in re-sealable freezer bags, with a bit of water, so you have them to hand whenever you need them (then they're as easy to use as tinned).

Put the pulses in a heavy-based saucepan, cover with cold water and leave to soak overnight. The next day, drain and rinse the pulses, return them to the pan and cover with cold water. Add a pinch of bicarbonate of soda and bring to the boil over a medium heat. Reduce the heat to low and simmer gently for 45 minutes–1 hour, until they are tender but retain a little bite. Take care to not overcook them, as they will quickly become mushy. Drain well, set aside the quantity needed for the recipe, and freeze the remaining pulses in batches, adding a little water to the freezer bags before sealing.

❧ ❧ ❧

Tip: Cook the beans at a low simmer and don't salt the cooking water (salting the water would turn them mushy).

HUMMUS

Serves 4

Everyone has a hummus these days, but this one is special. I learned the secrets of this super-smooth refined dip from a wonderful Lebanese chef. The first trick is to peel the chickpeas. The second is to add ice-cold water to smooth the dip at the end.

❧ ❧ ❧ ❧ ❧ ❧ ❧ ❧ ❧ ❧

325g (11½oz) cooked chickpeas
   (see opposite or use tinned)
2 garlic cloves, crushed
Juice of 1 lemon
4 tbsp extra virgin olive oil,
   plus extra for drizzling
4 tbsp tahini
2 tbsp ice-cold water
Salt and black pepper
Pimentón dulce (sweet paprika), to serve

To peel the chickpeas, fill a large bowl with cold water. Add the cooked chickpeas to the water in batches and gently rub them for 5 minutes to remove the skins and excess starch (do this with tinned chickpeas, too, if using). Skim off the skins, drain the bowl, refill and repeat at least twice to remove all the skins.

Place the skinned and drained chickpeas in the bowl of a food processor with the garlic, lemon juice, olive oil, tahini and ice-cold water, and season with salt and pepper. Whizz for 5–7 minutes until very smooth and light in colour (alternatively, blend in a high-sided container with a hand-held blender). Add more cold water if necessary, so the hummus blends freely. Taste and season again with salt and pepper, whizzing again to combine.

Hummus is done when it turns a shade or two paler as the cold water is added. Transfer to a bowl, drizzle with olive oil and sprinkle with pimentón dulce to serve.

❧ ❧ ❧

Tip: Use toasted sesame seed tahini with the consistency of thick crêpe batter.

CUCUMBER AND ONION PICKLES

Can Riero guests go wild over these, so we make these in spring with the abundance of cucumbers. They are great on burgers and sandwiches of all kinds, and with cheese and charcuterie boards. Best of all, great with falafel, hummus and cabbage slaw (see page 219). Absolutely delicious and easy to make, they make a brilliant impression.

❧ ❧ ❧ ❧ ❧ ❧ ❧ ❧ ❧ ❧ ❧

You will need: 3 x 500ml (18fl oz) sterilised glass jars (see page 295)

1kg (2lb 2oz) unwaxed pickling cucumbers, cut into 0.5cm (¼in) thick rounds
4 large sweet onions, cut into 0.5cm (¼in) thick rings
240g (8½oz) coarse salt
600ml (1 pint) white wine vinegar
600g (1¼lb) caster sugar
6 dried bird's eye chillies
1 tbsp yellow mustard seeds
1 tbsp black mustard seeds
1 tbsp coriander seeds
1 tbsp cumin seeds
1 tbsp whole black peppercorns

Combine the cucumbers, onions and salt in a large stainless steel bowl. Mix to coat the vegetables with the salt, add water to cover and set aside at room temperature for 4 hours.

Rinse the excess salt off the cucumbers and onions and place them on clean tea towels to drain.

Combine the vinegar, sugar and spices in a large stainless steel saucepan and bring to the boil. Reduce the heat and simmer for 20 minutes, to dissolve the sugar and infuse the vinegar with the spices, then add the drained cucumbers and onions and return to a simmer. Reduce the heat to low and simmer for 2–3 minutes, then remove it from the heat. Transfer the pickles and the pickling liquid to the sterilised jars, dividing the cucumbers, onions and chillies evenly among the jars, then seal and store.

MEMBRILLO (QUINCE PASTE)

Makes about 1.5kg (3lb 4oz) paste

Homemade membrillo is magnificent, dark orangey red, and sweet, with a gorgeous flowery scent. Sliced and beautifully wrapped, it makes an impressive gift. It is a beautiful addition to charcuterie boards and pairs especially well with Manchego curado.

❧ ❧ ❧ ❧ ❧ ❧ ❧ ❧ ❧ ❧ ❧

You will need: 23 x 13 x 7cm non-stick loaf tin

2kg (4lb 4oz) quince, cored and quartered (unpeeled)
2 lemons, halved
About 2kg (4lb 4oz) caster sugar

Line the base and sides of the loaf tin with baking parchment. Rub the cut sides of the quince with lemon, to stop them from browning. Put the quince in a large, heavy-based saucepan. Cover with cold water, bring to the boil, then simmer, uncovered, for 40–45 minutes, until the quince are very tender. Drain well and discard the cooking liquid.

Put the quince pulp in a bowl, break it up with a fork then pass it through a food mill to make a fine pulp.

Weigh the quince pulp, and for each 240g (8½oz) of quince measure out 220g (8oz) of sugar, and place both the sugar and quince pulp in a heavy-based saucepan. Grate the zest of the lemons into the pan and squeeze in the juice. Cook over a very low heat for about 10 minutes, or until the sugar has dissolved and iscompletely incorporated with the pulp. Increase the heat to medium-low and cook the mixture for 1–1½ hours, stirring continuously with a wooden scraper and making sure the mixture doesn't stick to the bottom of the pan and burn. Reduce the heat if it bubbles too much. The colour will deepen to a gorgeous burnt orange as it thickens. It is done when it reaches the texture of a thick paste that has to be shaken off the spoon.

Recipe continued overleaf

Spoon the quince into the prepared tin, smooth the surface with a spatula or the back of a spoon then set aside at room temperature and allow to cool completely. Once cool, run the blade of a sharp knife around the inside edge of the tin and turn the quince paste out onto a sheet of baking parchment. Slice it to the desired thickness and wrap each slice tightly in baking parchment or greaseproof paper, and wrap in clingfilm. Store it in the fridge for up to 10 months.

SAMFAINA JAM
Makes approximately 300g (11oz)

❧ ❧ ❧ ❧ ❧ ❧ ❧ ❧ ❧ ❧ ❧

500g (1lb 2oz) stage one *Samfaina* (see page 195)
1 fresh red chilli, deseeded and finely chopped
½ tsp aged sherry vinegar
Salt and black pepper

Stir the chilli into the *samfaina* and cook it for 1–1½ hours, uncovered, over a very low heat. Use a flame tamer or heat diffuser to slow the cooking down, if necessary. When it reaches the consistency of jam, remove it from the heat, add the sherry vinegar and season to taste.

FIG CHUTNEY
Makes 2 litres (3½ pints)

Ibiza figs are very sweet and juicy. If using conventional figs, taste the mixture while it cooks and add another 50g (2oz) sugar and 50ml (2fl oz) vinegar if you think it needs it. The chutney should be sweet, pungent and spicy.

❧ ❧ ❧ ❧ ❧ ❧ ❧ ❧ ❧ ❧ ❧

You will need: 4 x 500ml (18fl oz) sterilised glass jars (see page 295)

1½ tsp whole cloves, toasted and crushed in a mortar and pestle
1½ tsp allspice berries, toasted and crushed in a mortar and pestle
2kg (4lb 4oz) fresh green or black figs, quartered
325ml (11½fl oz) red wine vinegar
5 sweet white onions, thinly sliced
225g (8oz) soft light brown sugar
2 tbsp grated fresh ginger
4 dried bird's eye chillies
1 tsp yellow mustard seed
1 tsp black mustard seed
1 cinnamon stick
Large pared strips of peel from 1 lemon
Large pinch salt

Place all the ingredients in a saucepan or preserving pan with 1–1½ teaspoons of the clove and allspice mixture and bring to a simmer over a medium-high heat. Reduce the heat to low and simmer, uncovered, for 1–1½ hours, stirring occasionally, until the mixture reaches a jam-like consistency. Transfer to sterilised jars (see page 295)and seal. The chutney will keep in the fridge for up to 6 months.

AIOLI

Makes 750g (1lb 10oz)

This is adapted from Can Caus, to me the most delicious egg-free aioli. It is the single most important sauce eaten on Ibiza and across Catalonia. It appears on every table in every home, café and restaurant. There are many opinions about how best to make it, and many recipes, but all recipes follow one of two methods: with egg or without. At Can Riero, we prefer to make a simple, egg-free aioli, using milk to create the emulsion and make the garlic creamy.

❧ ❧ ❧ ❧ ❧ ❧ ❧ ❧ ❧ ❧ ❧

20g (¾oz) peeled garlic cloves, rougly chopped
100ml (3½fl oz) whole milk
1 tbsp salt, plus extra to taste (if required)
200ml (7fl oz) sunflower oil
50ml (2fl oz) extra virgin olive oil
4 leaves flat leaf parsley, washed and roughly chopped (optional)
Freshly ground black pepper

Put the garlic, milk and salt in a deep bowl and combine the oils in a measuring jug.

Use a hand-held blender on low speed to blend the milk. The milk will begin to foam and thicken slightly.

Begin to pour the oil into the milk, very slowly, while you keep blending. The milk and oil will begin to emulsify. Continue to pour in the oil in a slow steady stream, not moving the hand blender, blending continuously for 2–3 minutes. Add the parsley if using and continue blending, moving the blender up and down, slowly and gently, to incorporate the emulsion at the bottom of the jug, for another minute. The aioli should be rich, smooth and the consistency of soured cream. Taste, and season with more salt if desired and a couple of cracks of black pepper.

MALTAISE

Makes 300g (11oz)

Maltaise, a citrusy variation of the classic Hollandaise, is a rich citrussy sauce that is divine with roasted vegetables. This recipe is adapted from Julia Child's inimitable *Mastering the Art of French Cooking*.

❧ ❧ ❧ ❧ ❧ ❧ ❧ ❧ ❧ ❧ ❧

4 egg yolks
Pinch sea salt
1 tbsp lemon juice
3–4 tbsp orange juice
45g (1½oz) cold butter, cut into 6 lumps
175g (6oz) butter, melted
Finely grated zest of 1 orange
Salt and black pepper

Beat the egg yolks and salt in a metal bowl with a hand-held electric mixer until the yolks are thick and pale. Beat in the lemon juice and 1½ tablespoons of the orange juice. Place the bowl over a pan of barely simmering water (making sure the bottom of the bowl doesn't touch the water, as the eggs will cook and make the sauce lumpy) and heat for 3–5 minutes, whisking continuously, until the mixture thickens slightly.

Beat the chunks of butter into the egg yolk mixture one at a time, completely incorporating each lump before adding the next. The sauce will continue to thicken and will form an emulsion. Once the cold butter is completely incorporated, pour in the melted butter very slowly, beating continuously. If the sauce starts to split, remove the bowl from the heat and beat in another egg yolk. Beat in the remaining orange juice, 1 tablespoon at a time, until the sauce is nearly but not quite as thick as mayonnaise, then beat in the orange zest. Season to taste and cover the surface of the Maltaise with clingfilm to stop a skin forming. Chill until ready to serve.

PICANTE YOGHURT SAUCE

Makes 350g (12oz)

Yoghurt sauce not only has infinite variations, but pairs well with nearly everything we eat at Can Riero, from pork, beef and lamb to falafel, grilled vegetables or as a sandwich spread. The acid in the yoghurt cuts through the fattiness of meat, and adds a creamy coolness to everything else. We vary the vegetables according to the season, using cucumber in the warm months and radishes when it's cold. But feel free to try any vegetables you like.

❧ ❧ ❧ ❧ ❧ ❧ ❧ ❧ ❧ ❧ ❧ ❧

150g (5oz) full-fat plain bio yoghurt
2 small garlic cloves, crushed
2 small pickling cucumbers, peeled, topped and
   tailed or 1 salad cucumber, peeled, halved
   lengthways and deseeded
¼ sweet onion, peeled
1 tsp lemon juice
4 drops Habanero Hot Sauce (see page 284)
Salt and black pepper

Put the yoghurt in a medium bowl and add the garlic. Grate the cucumber and onion into the bowl using the large holes of a box grater, then add the remaining ingredients and mix to combine. Set aside at room temperature for about 30 minutes to allow the flavours to marry. Season to taste and serve (or chill until needed).

Variations
❧ Substitute 6 radishes, sliced into thin batons, for the cucumber.
❧ Add chopped coriander, parsley and basil, or a combination of all three.
❧ Use the grated zest from 1 lemon, instead of cucumber or radish.

ROASTED TOMATO SAUCE

Makes 2kg (4lb 4oz)

Roasted tomato sauce, with its lush texture and rich flavour, is our basic tomato sauce at Can Riero in the months when fresh tomatoes are out of season. As with all the basic recipes, it's worth making double the amount and freezing the leftovers. This roasted tomato sauce goes in everything from Barbecue Sauce (see page 61) to Aubergine Gratinada (see page 181).

❧ ❧ ❧ ❧ ❧ ❧ ❧ ❧ ❧ ❧ ❧ ❧

2 tbsp extra virgin olive oil
500g (1lb 2oz) onions, halved and sliced
   into 1cm (½ in) thick half moons
250g (9oz) red peppers (2 small or 1½ large),
   halved, deseeded and cut into thick batons
3 large garlic cloves, crushed
400g (14 oz) tin plum tomatoes
1 tbsp tomato paste
Roasting pan liquid (optional – see page 275)
Pinch brown sugar
1kg (2lb 2oz) Roasted Tomatoes (see page 275)
½ tsp sherry vinegar (optional)
Salt and black pepper

Heat the olive oil in a heavy-based frying pan over a medium-high heat, then add the onions, reduce the heat to low, add a pinch of salt and a couple of turns of the pepper mill, and fry slowly, uncovered, for 15–20 minutes, until the onions are soft and golden but not brown. Add the red pepper batons and garlic. Season again, then fry for 5–10 minutes until the peppers are soft. Add the tinned tomatoes, tomato paste and roasting pan liquid (if using), then add the sugar and cook for 5 minutes. Tip in the roasted tomatoes and cook, uncovered, for a further 20 minutes. Remove from the heat, season to taste and purée until smooth with a hand-held blender. The sauce should be smooth, deep red and vibrant in flavour. Return to a medium heat and cook for a further 5–10 minutes, then remove from the heat and taste. If necessary, add the sherry vinegar to lift the roasted tomato flavour. Season to taste.

ROMESCO SAUCE

Makes 400g (14oz)

Romesco is another sauce that is open to variation and everyone thinks his or her version is the best. My take is tasty: the spicy, smoky peppers play well against the velvety sweetness of the roasted vegetables and the richness of the almonds. Once tried, forever addicted.

❧ ❧ ❧ ❧ ❧ ❧ ❧ ❧ ❧ ❧ ❧

2 dried ñora chillies, split lengthways and deseeded
1 dried ancho chilli, split lengthways and deseeded
1 dried cayenne chilli, split lengthways and deseeded
4 garlic cloves, roughly chopped
50g (2oz) blanched almonds, toasted
    and roughly chopped
Small handful flat-leaf parsley, leaves
    stripped and stems discarded
1 slice white bread, fried in olive oil
4 Roasted Tomatoes (see page 275)
1 Roasted Red Pepper (see page 274)
4 tbsp extra virgin olive oil
1 tbsp sherry vinegar
Salt and black pepper

Place the chillies in a heatproof bowl, cover with hot water and leave to rehydrate for 30 minutes, then drain and roughly chop. Put the garlic and chillies in the bowl of a food processor and pulse until blended, then add the almonds, parsley and bread and pulse 2–3 times until the mixture comes together. Add the roasted tomatoes and pepper and pulse again, 3–4 times. The sauce should be thick and slightly coarse. Transfer the mixture to a bowl, add the olive oil and vinegar and combine with a rubber spatula. Season with salt, pepper and additional oil and vinegar to taste.

❧ ❧ ❧

Tip: Do not over-process the sauce, as the bread will become starchy if overworked, resulting in a gluey consistency.

ROASTED RED PEPPER SAUCE

Makes 3kg (6lb 6oz)

This sauce works well with either tinned or fresh tomatoes. Fresh tomatoes vary widely in sweetness and water content, and regular, non-organic tomatoes tend to be drier and less sweet. If additional liquid is needed, add 1 teaspoon of tomato paste per 120ml (4½fl oz) of water for flavour. The sauce is great on the *Bocadillo de Albóndigas* (see page 229), and is an essential component of Roasted Aubergine, Red Pepper and Fennel with Burrata (see page 178).

❧ ❧ ❧ ❧ ❧ ❧ ❧ ❧ ❧ ❧ ❧

3 tbsp extra virgin olive oil
1kg (2lb 2oz) onions, peeled, halved lengthways
    and thinly sliced
2 tsp demerara sugar
1 tsp salt
1 tsp freshly ground black pepper
2kg (4lb 4oz) plum tomatoes or 2 x 400g (14oz) tins
    plum tomatoes
½–1 tsp sherry vinegar, to taste
2 tbsp tomato paste
1kg (2lb 2oz) Roasted Red Peppers, roughly chopped
    (see page 274)
Salt and black pepper

Heat the olive oil in a large, heavy-based saucepan, then add the onions, sugar, salt and pepper.

Cook over a low heat, uncovered, for 20–25 minutes until slightly golden, soft and sweet (but make sure they don't brown).

Meanwhile, peel the tomatoes if you are using fresh tomatoes. Prepare a large bowl of iced water. Bring a saucepan of water to the boil. Cut a cross at the base of each tomato, just piercing the skin, not the flesh, then add them to the pan of boiling water. Cook for 1 minute, then remove using a slotted spoon and plunge them straight into the bowl of iced water until cool. The skin will curl up along the cuts and should slip off easily. Cut the peeled fresh tomatoes into chunks and add them to the fried onions.

Recipe continued overleaf

If using tinned tomatoes, gently break up the tomatoes in the tins then add them to the onions. Season to taste with salt, pepper and sherry vinegar then add the tomato paste. Continue to cook the sauce over a medium-low heat for 20 minutes, until the tomatoes have broken down and are incorporated with the onions. If the sauce gets too dry add a little water. Add the roasted red peppers and cook for 30–35 minutes, until the sauce is a deep red colour. Purée briefly with a hand-held blender (you don't want the sauce to be completely smooth) and return to the heat. Cook over a low heat for a further 20 minutes. The sauce should look like a deep red, rich tomato sauce. If it is too thick, add a little more water with another teaspoon of tomato paste and cook for a further 10 minutes to incorporate. Remove from the heat and season to taste. The sauce should have a vibrant red pepper flavour. If not, add half a teaspoon of vinegar, which will brighten the flavour.

HABANERO HOT SAUCE
Makes 300ml (11fl oz)

We grow a few different kinds of hot peppers at Can Riero. We started because I fell in love with the homemade strands hanging in local market stalls and I wanted to make my own. And so it began. Now they are integral to our way of cooking. We string them in autumn and make different kinds of hot sauce, pickles and an astonishingly hot flavoured olive oil. This recipe is particularly useful. Hot on its own, it can be mixed with yoghurt or crème fraîche for a milder sauce.

❦ ❦ ❦ ❦ ❦ ❦ ❦ ❦ ❦ ❦ ❦

You will need: 300ml (11fl oz) sterilised
   glass jar (see page 295)

10 fresh habanero chillies, deseeded and chopped
   (wear gloves if you have sensitive skin as they
   are very hot!)
4 carrots, sliced
1 onion, sliced
350ml (12fl oz) white wine vinegar
60ml (2½fl oz) lemon or lime juice
5 garlic cloves, crushed
2 tsp salt

Place all the ingredients in a saucepan and bring to a simmer. Cook over a medium heat for 8–10 minutes, until the vegetables are tender, then remove from the heat. Purée with a hand-held blender, then strain through a sieve or put through a food mill, if desired. Transfer to a sterilised jar. The sauce will keep for up to 1 year, sealed, and up to 6 months in the fridge once opened.

❦ ❦ ❦

Tip: Use rubber gloves when handling the peppers and be careful not to touch eyes, face, ears or anything sensitive. The burn is painful.

PAN CON TOMATE

Serves 2–3

There is something quite delicious about the simple combination of bread, tomato, oil and salt. On Ibiza, *Pan con Tomate* is eaten for breakfast, as an accompaniment to ham, cheese, sausages or anchovies, or with other tapas. In some parts of Catalonia diners are presented with a basket of delicious white rustic, thick-sliced toasted bread, a whole ripe red tomato, extra virgin olive oil and coarse sea salt so that they can assemble the dish themselves. Sometimes garlic is rubbed on the bread before the tomato. My version has garlic, but just a hint. The key to successful *Pan con Tomate* is the coarse sea salt. Sprinkle it over the prepared bread: the salt crystals are miraculous with the tomato and the slight crunch of bread.

❧ ❧ ❧ ❧ ❧ ❧ ❧ ❧ ❧ ❧ ❧ ❧

1 garlic clove, very thinly sliced
4 tbsp extra virgin olive oil, plus extra
    for drizzling
1 ciabatta or baguette, halved lengthways
1 salad tomato, or 2 tbsp Grated Tomato
    (see page 275)
Coarse salt and black pepper

Turn on the oven grill to medium. Add the garlic and a pinch of salt and pepper to the oil in a bowl and set it aside for 15 minutes to macerate.

Drizzle the cut side of each half of bread with some of the garlicky oil, and grill them crust side up for 2–3 minutes, until golden, then turn them over and grill cut-side up for a further 2–3 minutes until crunchy and golden.

Halve the tomato and rub it cut side down on the bread to lightly coat the bread with tomato pulp. Or spread the grated tomato evenly on the bread.

To serve, sprinkle the bread with salt and pepper, drizzle with more of the garlicky olive oil and cut into thirds on the diagonal.

PASTEL DE MANTEQUILLA

Serves 8–10

This recipe was inspired by the rich, moist cake our neighbour made and sold at a local shop. When she got older and could only make it to order, I had to create my own version. Although a joy to make, I miss the ritual of visiting the shop to buy a slice.

❧ ❧ ❧ ❧ ❧ ❧ ❧ ❧ ❧ ❧ ❧

You will need: 23cm (9in) round springform cake tin

200g (7oz) unsalted butter, softened,
    plus extra for greasing
225g (8oz) caster sugar
1 tsp vanilla extract
4 eggs, at room temperature
225g (8oz) self-raising flour, sifted,
    plus extra for dusting
50g (2oz) plain Greek yoghurt

Preheat the oven to 180°C (350°F), gas mark 4. Grease the base and sides of the tin with butter and dust with flour. Line the base with baking parchment and grease the parchment.

Cream together the butter, sugar and vanilla in the bowl of a stand mixer at medium-high speed until pale, light and fluffy, or in a bowl with a hand-held electric whisk. The sugar should be mostly worked in, with a slightly grainy texture. Add the eggs, one at a time, beating well after each. Remove the bowl from the stand and fold in the flour and yoghurt in three stages, taking care not to knock too much air out of the batter. The batter should slide easily off a spoon: if it is too thick add a little more yoghurt. Pour into the tin and level with a spatula. Knock the base of the pan on the work surface to remove any air bubbles. Bake for 30–35 minutes until golden, risen and springy to the touch; it is done when a toothpick inserted into the middle comes out clean. Remove from the oven. Cool it in the tin for 15 minutes, then remove to a wire rack to cool completely.

❧ ❧ ❧

Variation: For Baked Alaska (see page 261) reduce all the ingredient quantities by half.

ITALIAN MERINGUE

This is a wonderfully versatile dessert ingredient. Combine it with curds, use it to top pies and cakes, or bake it into meringues. The hot sugar syrup stabilises the meringue and gives it a thick, silky texture and beautiful glossy finish.

✣ ✣ ✣ ✣ ✣ ✣ ✣ ✣ ✣ ✣ ✣

4 egg whites, at room temperature
Pinch salt
200g (7oz) caster sugar

Put the egg whites in the clean bowl of a stand mixer fitted with the whisk attachment and break them up at a low speed. When the egg whites are beginning to come together, add the salt. Increase the speed to medium-high and beat for 3–5 minutes, until the mixture forms soft peaks, then turn off the machine.

Put the sugar and 100ml (3½fl oz) water in a small, heavy-based saucepan, preferably with a pouring spout, and put in a sugar thermometer. Cook over a medium heat for 6–9 minutes, until it reaches 115°C (240°F), then remove from the heat. Swirl the pan to redistribute the mixture if the sugar starts to burn, but do not stir it.

Turn the mixer back on and set the whisk at medium speed. Pour the hot sugar mixture down the side of the bowl in a gradual, steady stream. Once all the syrup is incorporated, increase the speed to medium-high. Beat for 5–8 minutes until the mixture is glossy and the peaks hold their form. To test, stop the mixer and lift the whisk out. The peaks should hold their form as it is lifted. Use the meringue mixture immediately.

✣ ✣ ✣

Tip: Wash and dry the bowl and whisk of the mixer carefully before use and ensure there is no yolk in the egg whites, as any impurities can ruin the structure of the meringue. Crack the eggs into a cup so if any yolk gets in you can set it aside and use a fresh egg.

STABILISED WHIPPED CREAM

Stabilising whipped cream extends the length of time it will hold its shape without weeping liquid or breaking down. It's ideal in the Café con Leche Roulade (see page 207) as it helps the cake hold its shape.

✣ ✣ ✣ ✣ ✣ ✣ ✣ ✣ ✣ ✣ ✣

1 tsp powdered gelatine
360ml (12fl oz) whipping cream, chilled
1 tsp vanilla extract
2–4 tbsp caster sugar

Put the gelatine in a bowl with 1½ tablespoons of cold water and leave it to soften for 5 minutes.

Meanwhile, whip the cream in the bowl of a stand mixer fitted with the whisk attachment on medium speed for 2–3 minutes, or in a mixing bowl with a hand-held electric whisk, until the whisk leaves a light trail in the cream. Reduce the speed to medium-low, add the vanilla extract and 2 tablespoons of the sugar, and beat to combine. Stop the mixer, taste the cream and add more sugar if desired, beating briefly to combine.

Add 1½ tablespoons of boiling water to the gelatine mixture and stir to dissolve it completely. Turn the mixer or whisk to medium speed and pour the gelatine liquid down the side of the bowl in a steady stream. Whisk the cream for 3–4 minutes at medium speed, until peaks hold when the whisk is lifted.

PRESERVED LEMONS

Makes 1 litre (1¾ pints) jar

We use preserved lemon rind to add a fantastic punch of citrus flavour to soups and stews. Finely chopped, it is equally delicious with roasted vegetables or sprinkled over winter fruit compote.

❧ ❧ ❧ ❧ ❧ ❧ ❧ ❧ ❧ ❧ ❧ ❧

You will need: 1 litre (1¾ pints) sterilised preserving jar with lid (see page 295)

7 lemons
1kg (2lb 2oz) coarse sea salt
2 tbsp white caster sugar

Juice 2 of the lemons and scrub the remaining 5 lemons, then mix the salt and sugar together in a large bowl and set aside.

Place the scrubbed lemons on a work surface stem end down and, using a sharp paring knife, slice three-quarters of the way down each lemon. Repeat, cutting each lemon into eighths, but being careful to leave the base intact. Spoon the salt mixture between the cuts, stuffing the lemons and pressing the salt down to the base of the cuts, then pour enough of the remaining salt mixture into the jar to completely cover the bottom. Pack the lemons tightly into the jar, adding extra salt to fill any spaces and cover the lemons. Seal the jar and leave for 6–8 hours at room temperature to soften, then open the jar and press the lemons down into the jar. Top with enough lemon juice and salt and sugar mixture to submerge them. Check the lemons every few hours to ensure they are covered with salt and juice, adding more if necessary, then seal and store at room temperature. The lemons are ready after about 3–4 weeks, when the skin is soft and pale. Once opened, keep the jar in the fridge (the lemons will keep well for up to 6 months).

LEMON CURD

Makes approximately 250ml (9fl oz)

Citrus curd, retro as it is, brings vibrant colour and flavour to the kitchen. To me it is the very taste of sunshine. We grow a wide variety of citrus fruits at Can Riero and make curd from many of them. The amount of sugar and zest we use varies depending on the fruit, but the basic method is similar. Curd is divine spooned from a jar, spread on buttered toast, used as a filling for a cake or as a base for parfait.

❧ ❧ ❧ ❧ ❧ ❧ ❧ ❧ ❧ ❧ ❧ ❧

You will need: 250ml (9fl oz) sterilised preserving jar with lid (see page 295)

1 large egg
3 egg yolks
110g (4oz) caster sugar
Pinch salt
90ml (3½fl oz) lemon juice
2–3 tbsp finely grated lemon zest
90g (3½oz) unsalted butter,
    cut into lumps

Whisk the egg and yolks in a medium stainless steel bowl to break them up. Add the sugar, salt, lemon juice and zest and whisk well.

Bring 200ml (7fl oz) water to a gentle simmer in a small saucepan and place the bowl over the pan. Whisk the egg mixture, adding the butter one lump at a time, until it is completely incorporated. Continue whisking over a medium heat for 10–12 minutes, until the curd is thick enough to hold the lines of the whisk.

Remove the bowl from the pan, cover the surface of the curd with clingfilm to prevent a skin forming, and allow to cool to room temperature. Store in a sterilised glass jar. It will keep, in the fridge, for up to 1 week.

❧ ❧ ❧

Tip: Do not let the bottom of the bowl touch the simmering water, as the eggs are likely to scramble. If the eggs do scramble, carry on thickening until the curd is set, then pass the curd through a fine-mesh sieve and serve. Curd is forgiving as well as divine.

BLOOD ORANGE CURD

Makes approximately 250ml

✣ ✣ ✣ ✣ ✣ ✣ ✣ ✣ ✣ ✣ ✣

You will need: 250ml (9fl oz) sterilised
  preserving jar with lid (see page 295)

160ml (5½fl oz) freshly squeezed orange juice
1 large egg
3 egg yolks
50g (2oz) caster sugar
Pinch salt
Juice of ½ lemon
1½ tbsp finely grated orange zest
50g (2oz) unsalted butter, cut into lumps

Put half of the orange juice in a small
saucepan and simmer for 8–10 minutes until
it has reduced by about half, then remove
from the heat.

Whisk the egg and yolks in a medium
stainless steel bowl to break them up. Add
the sugar, salt, remaining orange juice,
lemon juice and zest and whisk well.

Bring 200ml (7fl oz) water to a gentle
simmer in a small saucepan and place the bowl
over the pan. Whisk the egg mixture, adding
the butter one lump at a time, until it is
completely incorporated. Continue whisking
over a medium heat for 10–12 minutes, until
the curd is thick enough to hold the lines
of the whisk.

Remove the bowl from the pan, then add the
reduced orange juice to the finished curd, a little
at a time, until you have achieved the desired
consistency. Cover the surface of the curd with
clingfilm, to prevent a skin forming, and allow
to cool to room temperature. Store in a
sterilised glass jar. It will keep, in the fridge,
for up to 1 week.

PINK GRAPEFRUIT CURD

Makes approximately 250ml

✣ ✣ ✣ ✣ ✣ ✣ ✣ ✣ ✣ ✣ ✣

You will need: 250ml (9fl oz) sterilised
  preserving jar with lid (see page 295)

100ml (3½fl oz) freshly squeezed
  grapefruit juice
1 large egg
3 egg yolks
60g (2½oz) caster sugar
Pinch salt
2 tbsp finely grated grapefruit zest
50g (2oz) unsalted butter, cut into lumps

Put half of the grapefruit juice in a small
saucepan and simmer for 8–10 minutes until
it has reduced by about half, then remove
from the heat.

Whisk the egg and yolks in a medium
stainless steel bowl to break them up. Add
the sugar, salt, remaining grapefruit juice
and zest and whisk well.

Bring 200ml (7fl oz) water to a gentle
simmer in a small saucepan and place the bowl
over the pan. Whisk the egg mixture, adding
the butter one lump at a time, until it is
completely incorporated. Continue whisking
over a medium heat for 10–12 minutes, until
the curd is thick enough to hold the lines of
the whisk.

Remove the bowl from the pan, then add
the reduced grapefruit juice to the finished
curd, a little at a time, until you have achieved
the desired consistency. Cover the surface of
the curd with clingfilm, to prevent a skin
forming, and allow to cool to room temperature.
Store in a sterilised glass jar. It will keep, in
the fridge, for up to 1 week.

ACCOMPANIMENTS

BABY BROAD BEANS WITH CUMIN

Serves 6

Broad beans and toasted cumin complement each other completely, and are sublime when served with slow-roasted lamb.

❧ ❧ ❧ ❧ ❧ ❧ ❧ ❧ ❧ ❧

2kg (4lb 4oz) fresh baby broad
    beans, shelled
120ml (4½fl oz) olive oil
2 tbsp cumin seeds, toasted and roughly
    ground in a mortar and pestle
Sea salt flakes and black pepper

Bring a medium saucepan of water to the boil over a high heat, add a pinch of salt and the shelled broad beans, reduce the heat to medium and simmer for 4–5 minutes or until *al dente*. Drain the broad beans and set aside. When the beans are cool to the touch peel the thin membrane away and put the tender beans back in the pan. Add the olive oil and ground cumin and reheat over a medium-low heat to combine the flavours. Season to taste and serve.

❧ ❧ ❧

Tip: Allow the beans to cool slightly before seasoning so the salt flakes stay intact. It really enhances the flavour.

BABY CARROTS

Serves 6

Though carrots are not common on Ibiza, there are a few Ibicenco farmers who grow them. Distinctively sweet and earthy, they are a real treat when available. Flat-leaf parsley and orange are the perfect flavours to make any carrot, conventional or local-grown, taste very special.

❧ ❧ ❧ ❧ ❧ ❧ ❧ ❧ ❧ ❧

700g (1½lb) whole baby carrots,
    tops cut leaving 1cm (½in) of the
    green tops, peeled
1 tbsp extra virgin olive oil
2 tbsp unsalted butter
1 tsp soft light brown sugar
Finely grated zest of ½ orange
Small handful flat-leaf parsley,
    leaves chopped
Salt and black pepper

Steam the carrots for 8–10 minutes until *al dente*. Remove from the heat and set aside.

Heat the olive oil and butter in a frying pan over a medium heat and add the brown sugar, a pinch of salt and a pinch of pepper. Add the carrots and toss with tongs until well coated. Add the orange zest and toss again, then add the parsley, toss quickly to incorporate and remove from the heat. Season to taste before serving.

CARROT AND RED CABBAGE SLAW

Serves 4

Vegetable slaws, fresh and crunchy, make great winter salads. Kohlrabi, broccoli stem, beetroot and cabbage of all kinds make great variations. For a more flavourful slaw, make ahead and set it aside for 30 minutes or so to give it time to absorb the dressing.

❧ ❧ ❧ ❧ ❧ ❧ ❧ ❧ ❧ ❧ ❧

175g (6oz) carrots, coarsely grated
175g (6oz) red cabbage, grated or thinly
    sliced using a mandoline
½ red onion, thinly sliced
1 yellow pepper, deseeded and cut into
    thin batons
4 tbsp extra virgin olive oil
1 tbsp orange juice
1 tsp grated orange zest
2 tbsp aged sherry vinegar
1½ tsp runny honey
1 tsp salt
¾ tsp freshly ground black pepper

Combine all the vegetables in a bowl.

Put the olive oil, orange juice and zest, vinegar, honey, salt and pepper in a jar or bottle, seal and shake vigorously until well combined.

Toss the vegetables with the dressing and season to taste. Set aside at room temperature for 30 minutes or more (maximum 2 hours) to allow the flavours to marry before serving.

GRILLED VEGETABLES

Serves 6

Grilled vegetables are the perfect accompaniment to skirt steak; the vibrant colours and meaty textures make for a great plate.

❧ ❧ ❧ ❧ ❧ ❧ ❧ ❧ ❧ ❧ ❧

4 tbsp marinade from the entraña
    (see page 119)
3 courgettes, cut lengthways into
    ½cm (¼in) thick slices
6 salad tomatoes, halved
2 large yellow peppers,
    deseeded and cut in eighths
1 large aubergine, cut lengthways
    in 1cm (½in) thick slices
1–2 tbsp extra virgin olive oil (optional)
Salt and black pepper

Put 2 tablespoons each of the marinade in 2 resealable freezer bags and divide the sliced vegetables between the bags. Seal and shake well to coat the vegetables in the marinade. Add 1–2 tablespoons of olive oil if necessary, to get them nice and juicy. Transfer the bags to the fridge to marinate for 1–2 hours, or overnight.

Preheat a barbecue grill or griddle pan to very hot. Grill the tomatoes for 3–4 minutes on each side, and the peppers, aubergine and courgettes for 2–3 minutes on each side, until the vegetables are charred and tender, but not burnt. Transfer to a serving plate.

PITA BREAD

Makes 6

Homemade pita is delicious and impressive, yet dead easy to make. The trick is to work the dough lightly so you don't overdevelop the gluten. A light touch makes for a tender pita. Bake them on a very hot tray in a very hot oven to achieve a good puff.

✤ ✤ ✤ ✤ ✤ ✤ ✤ ✤ ✤ ✤ ✤

300ml (11fl oz) tepid water
7g packet (2¼ tsp) dried yeast
1 tsp runny honey
65g (2½oz) stoneground wholewheat flour
400g (14oz) plain white flour,
   plus extra for dusting
Olive oil, for greasing
1 tsp fine sea salt

Combine the tepid water with the yeast, honey, wholewheat flour and 50g (2oz) of the white flour in a bowl and set aside. The mixture should begin to froth within 3–4 minutes. Add the remaining flour and the salt, mix well and bring the mixture together with your hands to form a rough dough.

Knead the dough gently for about 3 minutes, or until the dough is soft, then place it in a greased bowl. Cover the bowl with a clean tea towel and leave the dough to rest for 15 minutes, then remove from the bowl, knead for a further 2 minutes until the dough is smooth, and shape it into a ball and place it back into the greased bowl. Cover the bowl again and leave the dough to rise at room temperature for 1–1½ hours, until it has doubled in size. Preheat the oven to 220°C (430°F), gas mark 7, and put a baking tray in the oven to heat up.

Once risen, remove the dough from the bowl and gently knock back the dough. Divide it into 6 equal pieces, then roll each piece out into 25cm (10in) rounds on a lightly floured work surface.

Remove the baking tray from the oven and place 2 dough rounds onto the hot baking tray. Bake for 2–3 minutes, waiting until the pitas puff up before opening the oven door. Use tongs to turn the pitas over and bake them for a further 2–3 minutes, until golden, puffed up and cooked through. Remove the pitas from the oven, wrap them in a tea towel to keep warm, reheat the baking tray and repeat until all the dough rounds are cooked.

PIMIENTOS DE PADRÓN

Serves 6

Pimientos de Padrón are hugely popular on Ibiza, particularly with grilled food. They are great eaten with a glass of wine while you're grilling the rest of the dinner. Eating them can be surprising: both spicy and mild peppers grow on the same bush and are indistinguishable, but some are hot, others not; it's a delicious game of roulette.

✤ ✤ ✤ ✤ ✤ ✤ ✤ ✤ ✤ ✤ ✤

2–3 tbsp extra virgin olive oil
400g (14oz) fresh Pimientos de Padrón
Salt flakes

Heat the olive oil in a large heavy-based frying pan until very hot. Tip in the pimientos. There should be enough space to scorch them on the hot base of the pan (cook them in two batches if necessary), while tossing them. Continue shaking and cooking for 5–6 minutes, until the skins char to a brown colour. Transfer to a serving platter and sprinkle with salt flakes. If serving from a bowl, sprinkle salt between each layer. Serve immediately.

PATATAS BRAVAS

Serves 4

Patatas Bravas, crispy potatoes with a spicy sauce, are a wonderful, hugely popular tapa. Traditionally they are deep fried but we oven-bake them because we like to eat them more often than we can justify deep-frying. Cook them twice, once at a lower heat to cook through, then a high heat roast to crisp. Don't skimp on the olive oil, the potatoes need a fair amount to get crunchy.

✤ ✤ ✤ ✤ ✤ ✤ ✤ ✤ ✤ ✤ ✤

800g (1¾lb) Maris Piper potatoes, cut into wedges lengthways, skin on (about 16 wedges per potato)
½ head garlic, cloves peeled and smashed
Large handful rosemary leaves
Handful thyme leaves
80ml (3¼fl oz) extra virgin olive oil
Salt and black pepper

Bravas sauce
80g (3¼oz) crème fraîche
40g (1½oz) plain yoghurt
1 tbsp Habanero Hot Sauce (see page 284)

Preheat the oven to 180°C (350°F), gas mark 4.

Toss the potato wedges, garlic and herbs with the olive oil and some salt and pepper. Divide them between 2 baking trays and bake for 30–40 minutes, until crispy on the outside and tender inside. Halfway through cooking, remove the trays from the oven and scrape and toss the potatoes, and swap the pans around when you return them to the oven, so they cook evenly. Remove from the oven and turn on the oven grill to hot. Grill each tray of wedges for 5–6 minutes, turning the wedges once, until they are very crunchy.

To make the bravas sauce, mix the crème fraîche, yoghurt and hot sauce in a bowl. Season to taste with salt and pepper.

IBICENCO FRIED POTATOES

Serves 6 as a side dish

Fried potatoes with garlic and peppers are a traditional dish on Ibiza. Pair them with aioli (see page 281).

✤ ✤ ✤ ✤ ✤ ✤ ✤ ✤ ✤ ✤ ✤

600g (1¼lb) Maris Piper potatoes, peeled
1 litre (1¾ pints) light olive oil
½ each red and green pepper, deseeded and sliced into matchsticks
1 head garlic, cloves peeled and halved
Salt and black pepper

Slice the potatoes into paper-thin rounds, putting the slices in a bowl of iced water.

Put the oil and a thermometer in a large, deep heavy-based saucepan and heat the oil to 182°C (360°F).

Drain and dry the potato slices thoroughly. Mix the potatoes, peppers and garlic together in a bowl then divide them into 3 batches. Fry each batch in the oil for 3–4 minutes until lightly golden. Remove with a slotted spoon and transfer to a baking sheet lined with kitchen paper to drain.

Just before serving, fry the potatoes for a further 2–3 minutes until crisp and golden. Place on a baking sheet lined with fresh, clean kitchen paper to drain then serve immediately.

LARDER

A well-stocked larder is an essential component of fabulous fresh, seasonal cooking. With good-quality basics on hand all that's required to prepare a wonderful meal is a quick stop at the greengrocer, butcher or fishmonger to pick up fresh ingredients. Always buy the best quality provisions you can; a finished dish is the sum of its parts. The Can Riero larder may look luxurious, but sourcing fabulous authentic ingredients instantly improves the finished dish.

Cooking is a journey. I hope that after experiencing a taste of Ibiza, the Balearics and Spain through this book you'll be inspired to explore what is fabulously fresh, seasonal and local to you – wherever you are in the world.

- Aged Jerez sherry vinegar
- Red wine vinegar
- White wine vinegar
- Aged Modena balsamic vinegar
- White vinegar
- Brandy
- Sherry
- Serrano ham
- Black olives
- Polenta
- Pasta, various
- Haricot beans
- Chickpeas
- Garlic
- Onions
- Extra virgin olive oil
- Mustard powder
- Cinnamon sticks
- Whole nutmeg
- Cumin seeds
- Coriander seeds
- Whole star anise
- Dried bay leaves
- Sea salt – very coarse, coarse, fine and flaked
- Black peppercorns

STOCKISTS

The following delis sell a comprehensive range of Spanish products:

London
Brindisa Borough Market: The Floral Hall, Borough Market, Stoney St, London SE1 9AF; 020 7407 1036; www.brindisa.com/
Brindisa Food Rooms, Brixton: 41–43 Atlantic Road, Brixton, SW9 8JL; 0207 733 0634; www.brindisa.com/
R.Garcia and Sons: 248250 Portobello Rd, London W11 1LL; 020 7221 6119 http://rgarciaandsons.com/
Spandeli: 246 Dalston Lane, London E8 1LQ; 020 8985 3720; www.facebook.com/SpandeliUk/

Bristol
Viandas Spanish Deli: 12 Park Row, Bristol BS1 5LJ; 07927 573696; www.facebook.com/viandasukbristol/

Liverpool
Lunya: 18–20 College Lane, Liverpool 1, Liverpool, L1 3DS; 0151 706 9770; http://lunya.co.uk/

Manchester
Lunya: Barton Arcade, Deansgate, Manchester, M3 2BB; 0161 413 3317; http://lunya.co.uk/

General Stockists
Many speciality Spanish products are available in the following stores:
Fortnum and Mason: 181 Piccadilly, London, W1A 1ER; 020 7734 8040; www.fortnumandmason.com/
Harvey Nichols: Branches in Knightsbridge, Bristol, Manchester, Edinburgh, Birmingham, Leeds, Liverpool; www.harveynichols.com/
Selfridges Food Hall: Branches in London, Birmingham and Manchester; www.selfridges.com/GB/en/
Whole Foods: Branches in Camden, Cheltenham, Clapham Junction, Fulham, Giffnock, Kensington,Piccadilly Circus, Richmond, Stoke Newington; www.wholefoodsmarket.com/
Larger branches of Waitrose, Sainsbury's and Tesco also carry many of the speciality ingredients featured in this book.

The following products can also be
ordered via the web:

Brandied cherries
Griottines: www.griottines.co.uk
Cecina Ibergour: www.ibergour.co.uk/en
Eatapas: www.eatapas.co.uk/en/
The Tapas Lunch Co:
www.thetapaslunchcompany.co.uk/

Jerez sherry vinegar
Melbury and Appleton:
www.melburyandappleton.co.uk/
Sous Chef: www.souschef.co.uk/
Vinosofos: www.vinosofos.co.uk/

Mahón cheese
Delicioso: www.delicioso.co.uk/shop/
Eatapas Ltd: www.eatapas.co.uk/en/
Grey's Fine Foods: www.greysfinefoods.com/
Ibergour: www.ibergour.co.uk/en
Iberian Wines and Food:
www.iberianwinesandfood.com/
International Cheese:
www.internationalcheese.co.uk/
Melbury and Appleton:
www.melburyandappleton.co.uk/
Teddington Cheese Online:
www.teddingtoncheese.co.uk/

Manchego
Igourmet: www.igourmet.com/
Pong: www.pongcheese.co.uk/
The Tapas Lunch Co:
www.thetapaslunchcompany.co.uk/

Membrillo
Lola Espana: www.lolaespana.com/
Sous Chef: www.souschef.co.uk/
The Tapas Lunch Co:
www.thetapaslunchcompany.co.uk/

Padrón peppers
Fine Food Specialist:
www.finefoodspecialist.co.uk/
South Devon Chilli Farm:
www.southdevonchillifarm.co.uk/
The Tapas Lunch Co:
www.thetapaslunchcompany.co.uk/

Pata negra
Bellota: bellota.co.uk/
Fine Food Specialist:
www.finefoodspecialist.co.uk/
Jamonarium: www.jamonarium.com/en/
Spanish ham: www.spanishham.co.uk/
The Tapas Lunch Co:
www.thetapaslunchcompany.co.uk/
Wine and Ham: www.wineandham.com/

Pimentón dulce/picante/ahumado
Fine Food Specialist:
www.finefoodspecialist.co.uk/
Melbury and Appleton:
www.melburyandappleton.co.uk/
Sous Chef: www.souschef.co.uk/

Pistachio paste
Sous Chef: www.souschef.co.uk/

Queso fresco
The Tapas Lunch Co:
www.thetapaslunchcompany.co.uk/

Roasted peppers
Healthy Supplies:
www.healthysupplies.co.uk/

Serrano ham
Ibergour: www.ibergour.co.uk/en
Fine Food Specialist:
www.finefoodspecialist.co.uk/
Pure Spain: www.purespain.co.uk/
The Tapas Lunch Co:
www.thetapaslunchcompany.co.uk/
Ultracomida: www.ultracomida.co.uk/

Spanish olive oil
Made in Spain: madeinspain.uk/en/
Pure Spain: www.purespain.co.uk/
Spanish Olive Oil:
www.spanisholiveoil.co.uk/

Spanish sausages and charcuterie
Grey's Fine Foods: www.greysfinefoods.com/
Igourmet: www.igourmet.com/
The Tapas Lunch Co:
www.thetapaslunchcompany.co.uk/
Tom Hixson: www.tomhixson.co.uk/

INDEX

ACKNOWLEDGEMENTS

A cookbook is quite something to produce: research, shopping, cooking, testing, cooking again. Styling, shooting, sharpening, designing, covering – a lot of jobs, a lot of people and a lot of work. Fabulous fun, often frustrating, sometimes overwhelming. It has been a huge joy to bring the vision to life. There are many people to thank who have shared so generously their time, experience and knowledge over the last five years. It has been an honour to work with each and every one of them.

Special thanks to my family for infinite love, support and patience, I love you all.
My husband Rene and daughter Sofia for being there with me every step of the way.
My mom, Hallie Goelet, for all of the work, recipe testing and endless passionate food talk, it was a fantastic summer.
My dad, Michael Goelet, who would have loved to see this book in print.
My mother-in-law, Jannie Sijmonsbergen, much beloved.
My grandparents, Dennis and Ann Marie Maguire, for passing on the love of home-grown, local and organic food. They were organic farmers before anyone even knew what it meant.
My aunt and fabulous cook Alex Auti, for her awesome dessert advice.
Lynn and Arnie Feld for their support and enthusiasm.
Gigi and Flori Mierlacioiu, our wonderful support at Can Riero, we could not get by without them.
Tammy and Jr Newton.

Thanks to the *Eivissa* Crew for working with me, creating a real book from the vision: Neil Allen, David Munns and Victoria Allen, Andrew Jackson, Lizzie Harris, Flori Mierlacioiu, Leah Kamath, Cila Warncke (editor), Sally Riera (Spanish and Catalan language editor), Amanda Barokh (production coordinator) and Cat Milton.
And to my agent, Eugenie Furniss, for seeing the potential, and my publicist Tanya Layzell-Payne.
The HarperCollins crew: Emily Barrett, Georgina Atsiaris, Emily Arbis, Claire Ward, Julie MacBrayne, Hannah Gamon, Oli Malcolm, Jay Cochrane, Anna Derkacz, Monica Green, Alan Cracknell, Cliff Webb and Polly Osborn. And most especially Grace Cheetham, Publisher, for believing in the project and in me and for bringing it all to life. And to Emma and Alex at Smith & Gilmour.

Thanks to: María José Estrella for her wonderful friendship and help with historical research, Tim Payne, Pedro Cervero and Charles Vexenat from Bar 1805, Master of the cocktails, both, Ronnie Mussona for sharing both his fabulous farm and fabulous stories, Vicente Juan and Catalina Ferrer for teaching me about bees, bread, figs and everything Ibicenco. Carlos and Sarah from Cala Xuclar, Sally Riera for fact checking and mushroom foraging with her dad, Vicente Riera Planells, Juan Antonio Torres Marí for those wonderful hours spent fishing, Marchien Bakker for unfailing support, Tom Mollo for his gaucho juice and Pepe our fabulous paella chef. Vincente/Horse Country Club, Santa Gertrudis.

A huge thank you to the wonderful people from the Santa Eulària Market who have taught me a lot about Spanish, Catalan and Ibicenco food.
Carnicería Pepita y Emilio for fantastic Spanish meat and for explaining all the cuts.
Juan and María at Fruta María for their gorgeous market stall full of home-grown produce, endless advice on growing and trips to their farm.
Charcutería Ramís for huge amounts of information on Spanish cheese and cured meat.
Tani Fruit for beautiful Spanish speciality produce and the best wild mushrooms.

Thanks to the many food producers, vendors and restaurants and businesses for providing fabulous food, meals and places to stay, as well as infinite information and advice:
Victoria-Gasse, Galeria Elefante, for fabulous props.
Daniel Witte, Sal de Ibiza.
Frutos Secos, Ibiza, S.L..
Vicente Torres, Sal Torres.
Salinera Española.
Joan Benet, Olive oil.
Miquel Guash, Can Miquel Guasch.
Atzaro Agroturismo.
Toni, Chiringuito de Aguas Blancas.
Macao Restaurant – Sonia and Luca.
Es Torrent Restaurant.
Vista Alegre, Sant Joan.
Pescadería Sant Joan.
Benvenuto and Monica, Zero Gradi.
Pollo Martín.
Luigi Massimo, Casa Artina, the maker of the wonderful mozzarella and ricotta we use at Can Riero.
Can Bar Cosmi, Santa Agnès.
Can Caus, farm, restaurant and shop.
Los Pinos Playa Restaurant, Portinatx, chefs Maria and Vicente and their sons Juanito and Vicente.
Ca'n Guimo, Esteban and Carol.
Macao restaurant, Santa Gertrudis, Sonia and Luca.
Ca'n Marti, Agroturismo, Sant Joan.
Salifret, Santa Eulària.
El Pirata de Tortillo, Matteo.
Peix Sec, Formentera, David.
Consejo Queso Mahón, Menorca.
Binigarba Queso, Menorca.
Subaida, Menorca.
Agroturismo Ca Na Xini/Hort Sant Patrici, Menorca.

A final special thanks to the fabulous friends who have supported me, some of whom have lent a patient ear for endless food talk: Jenny and Naylor Stone, and Nancy Carleton for the early years in the kitchen, Sue Irving and Hilary Robinson, Marpessa, Scott and Ylwa Usher, Douglas and Delphine Edelman, Heti van Driest, George Kuijl and Noah Yalou Kuijl, Amanda Burton, Jane and John Veale, Annie Wilkes, Rebecca Frayn, Peter and Juliet Kindersley, Karyn Lewis, Luke and Michelle Pepe, Onita Moulik, Rachel Parsons, Joel Rice and José Jiménez Ortega, Annie Peel, Sophie Burton, Emily and Will Staab, Javier and Caroline Anadon, Elodie Wright, Jaume and Kristina Guasch.